Guidelines for Singleness and Marriage

Guidelines for Singleness and Marriage

by
John MacArthur, Jr.

WORD OF GRACE COMMUNICATIONS
P.O. Box 4000
Panorama City, CA 91412

All Scripture quotations, unless noted otherwise, are from the *New Scofield Reference Bible*, King James Version. Copyright © 1967 by Oxford University Press, Inc. Reprinted by permission.

Library of Congress Cataloging in Publication Data

MacArthur, John F.
  Guidelines for singleness and marriage.

  (John MacArthur's Bible studies)
  Includes index.
  1. Bible. N.T. Corinthians, 1st, VI, 12-VII, 40—Criticism, interpretation, etc. 2. Marriage—Biblical teaching. 3. Divorce—Biblical teaching. 4. Remarriage—Biblical teaching. I. Title. II. Series MacArthur, John F. Bible studies.
  BS2675.2.M287 1986   227'.206   86-21754
  ISBN 0-8024-5343-0 (pbk.)

1 2 3 4 5 6 7 Printing/GB/Year 91 90 89 88 87 86

Printed in the United States of America

Contents

These Bible studies are taken from messages delivered by Pastor-Teacher John MacArthur, Jr., at Grace Community Church in Panorama City, California. These messages have been combined into a 6-tape album entitled *Guidelines for Singleness and Marriage*. You may purchase this series either in an attractive vinyl cassette album or as individual cassettes. To purchase these tapes, request the album *Guidelines for Singleness and Marriage* or ask for the tapes by their individual GC numbers. Please consult the current price list; then, send your order, making your check payable to:

WORD OF GRACE COMMUNICATIONS
P.O. Box 4000
Panorama City, CA 91412

Or call the following number:
818-982-7000

1
Christian Liberty and Sexual Freedom

Outline

Introduction
A. The Conduct
   1. The morality defined
   2. The malice demonstrated
B. The Context
   1. The folly of division (chaps. 1-4)
   2. The failure of discipline (chap. 5)
   3. The futility of dissension (chap. 6:1-11)
   4. The fate of decadence (chap. 6:12-20)

Lesson
I. Sexual Sin Harms the Body (v. 12a)
   A. The Enticement of Sexual Sin
      1. Proverbs 5:3-6
      2. Proverbs 5:18-19
   B. The Elimination of Sexual Sin
      1. Proverbs 6:23-29
      2. Proverbs 7:4-8
      3. Proverbs 9:17-18
      4. 1 Corinthians 10:8
      5. Psalm 51:2-3
II. Sexual Sin Controls the Body (v. 12b)
   A. The Enslavement of Sexual Sin
   B. The Ending of Sexual Sin
      1. 1 Thessalonians 4:3-4
      2. Romans 8:13
      3. 1 Corinthians 9:26-27
   C. The Escalation of Sexual Sin
      1. Psalm 1:1
      2. James 1:13-15
      3. 2 Timothy 3:13
III. Sexual Sin Perverts the Body (vv. 13-20)

7

A. The Body Is for the Lord (vv. 13-14)
   1. The biological function
   2. The spiritual union
B. The Body Is a Member of Christ (vv. 15-18)
   1. The extent of sexual sin
   2. The evil of sexual sin
   3. The erasing of sexual sin
      a) Genesis 39:12
      b) 2 Timothy 2:22
   4. The examination of sexual sin
C. The Body Is a Temple of the Holy Spirit (vv. 19-20)
   1. 1 Peter 1:18-19
   2. 2 Corinthians 6:16

Introduction

In 1 Corinthians 6:12-20, the apostle Paul describes the biblical perspective of sexual morality. He gives the basis for Christian liberty and sexual freedom. And unless you know the Lord Jesus Christ, Christian morality will be hard to understand.

A. The Conduct

   1. The morality defined

      The Corinthian church had been taught by Paul that it is God's grace alone that saves and keeps one saved. God is the highest court, and He has declared that believers are righteous. There is no higher appeal. Yet the church at Corinth had rationalized their inappropriate sexual activity with a theological excuse. The Corinthian church thought that since they had been declared righteous because of their faith in Christ, they could sin without consequence. There are many religious people who say the same thing today. They say, "Everything is taken care of because Christianity has made us free, so let's live it up!" Other people say, "What's the big deal about sex? It's only a biological function." They look at their sexual freedom as if it were amoral.

   2. The malice demonstrated

      The Corinthian Christians lived in a city that was synonymous with illicit sex. The Greek work *korinthiazesthai*—to corinthianize—meant to live with drunken and immoral debauchery (William Barclay, *The Letters to the Corinthians* [Philadelphia: Westminster, 1975], pp. 2-3). The Corinthian Christians were overwhelmed with that kind of life-style. They assumed that since they were saved, it was all right to continue living a debauched life. They did not look at their sexual sin as anything serious but simply as a biological function.

B. The Context

The Corinthians were carrying their former life-style into the church. The problem of sexual immorality was simply another problem which the church at Corinth had to deal with. Paul wrote the entire epistle of 1 Corinthians to respond to each of the problems that resulted from their former life-style.

1. The folly of division (chaps. 1-4)

In 1 Corinthians 1-4, Paul deals with division in the church. They were divided over human leaders and philosophy. Both of those sins were carryovers from their former life.

2. The failure of discipline (chap. 5)

In 1 Corinthians 5, Paul deals with the evil of failing to discipline sin. That was a reflection of the Corinthians' tolerance toward sin.

3. The futility of dissension (chap. 6:1-11)

In 1 Corinthians 6:1-11, Paul deals with the sin of suing fellow believers. The Corinthian society was litigious, and the church simply carried that tendency over into their Christian life.

4. The fate of decadence (chap. 6:12-20)

The Corinthian believers were immoral before they came to Christ and carried that right into their Christian experience. Paul deals with their sin of immorality in 1 Corinthians 6:12-20 by taking apart their rationalization for thinking it was all right.

Lesson

I. SEXUAL SIN HARMS THE BODY (v. 12*a*)

"All things are lawful unto me, but all things are not expedient."

The apostle Paul says all things are possible within the area of God's grace but that not everything is expedient. The Greek word for "expedient" is *sumpherei*, which means "to profit." Paul in effect is saying, "God will forgive the believer's sin, but the price is high." Immorality is one of the things that God forgives, but there is a heavy price to pay. If you as a Christian commit immorality, God has forgiven you totally and completely by the blood of Jesus Christ, but there is harm built into that sin. No sin is ever right or good, and no sin ever produces anything right or good. Sin is never worthwhile. In the sense that believers are free and no longer under the penalty of the law in any way, all things are lawful for them. Yet sin never brings profit; it always brings loss.

A. The Enticement of Sexual Sin

No sin that a person commits has more built-in pitfalls than sexual sin. It has broken more marriages, shattered more homes, caused more heartache and disease, and destroyed more lives than alcohol and drugs combined.

1. Proverbs 5:3-6—"The lips of a strange woman drop as an honeycomb, and her mouth is smoother than oil, but her end is bitter as wormwood, sharp as a two-edged sword. Her feet go down to death; her steps take hold on sheol. Lest thou shouldest ponder the path of life, her ways are unstable, that thou canst not know them." The saying "What you see is what you get" is not necessarily true.

Solomon gives good advice in verses 7-9: "Hear me now therefore, O ye children, and depart not from the words of my mouth. Remove thy way far from her, and come not near the door of her house, lest thou give thine honor unto others, and thy years unto the cruel." Your chances of becoming involved in adultery are less if you stay away from places where adulterers are waiting.

When people get into compromising situations and fall, they lose their honor and self-respect. Instead of associating with honorable people, they wind up with cruel people. Solomon also says in verse 10, "Lest strangers be filled with thy wealth, and thy labors be in the house of an alien." A person could actually lose his fortune because he had been destroyed by sexual sin. Many men are saddled with paying alimony because of their sin. People have lost their lives and livelihood to immorality. Only when a person is old and has nothing but the pain and agony of his sin will he say, "How have I hated instruction, and my heart despised reproof; and have not obeyed the voice of my teachers, nor inclined mine ear to them that instructed me" (v. 12-13).

2. Proverbs 5:18-19—"Let thy fountain be blessed, and

10

rejoice with the wife of thy youth. Let her be as the loving hind and pleasant roe; let her breasts satisfy thee at all times, and be thou ravished always with her love." Solomon isn't saying God is against all sex. Sex is a wonderful thing as long as it occurs within the guidelines of marriage.

In verses 20-21, Solomon gives a contrast by saying, "Why wilt thou, my son, be ravished with a strange woman and embrace the bosom of a foreigner? For the ways of man are before the eyes of the Lord, and He ponders all his goings." Why does a Christian commit adultery when he knows the Lord is watching?

B. The Elimination of Sexual Sin

1. Proverbs 6:23-29,32—Solomon said, "The commandment is a lamp, and the law is light, and reproofs of instruction are the way of life, to keep thee from the evil woman, from the flattery of the tongue of a foreign woman. Lust not after her beauty in thine heart, neither let her take thee with her eyelids. For by means of an unchaste woman a man is brought to a piece of bread; and the adulteress will hunt for the precious life. Can a man take a fire in his bosom, and his clothes not be burned? So is he that goeth in to his neighbor's wife; whosoever toucheth her shall not be innocent." God's Word is the light that will keep you away from sexual immorality. "A foreign woman" simply means anyone other than your own wife.

As verse 26 attests, something as high and lofty as a man who is designed in the image of God is brought down to nothing but a piece of bread because of sexual immorality. Do you think you're going to commit sexual sin and get away with it? You're wrong. You can't take fire in your bosom without burning your clothes (v. 27). Verse 32 ends by saying, "Whoso committeth adultery with a woman lacketh understanding." It is foolish to commit adultery because "he that doeth it destroyeth his own soul" (v. 32). God may forgive the Christian for committing adultery but that doesn't make it the right or smart thing to do.

2. Proverbs 7:4-23—Solomon says, "Say unto wisdom, Thou art my sister, call understanding thy kinswoman, that they may keep thee from the strange woman, from the foreigner who flattereth with her words. For at the

window of my house I looked through my casement, and beheld among the simple ones, I discerned among the youths, a young man void of understanding, passing through the street near her corner; and he went the way to her house" (vv.4-8). Wisdom will keep you from women who flatter you. Solomon gives an illustration in verse 6. He looked through his window and saw an unwise young man. The world is full of unwise men. The old trade of prostitution hasn't changed much; prostitutes are still on street corners (v. 8). Here is an unwise man going down the street of a harlot.

He comes near her corner and "went the way to her house, in the twilight, in the evening, in the black and dark night" (vv. 8-9). Something like this usually occurs at night. Solomon says in verse 10, "Behold, there met him a woman with the attire of a harlot, and subtle of heart." You can usually tell a harlot by the way she dresses, not only in those days, but today as well. "She is loud and stubborn; her feet abide not in her house; now is she outside, now in the streets, and lieth in wait at every corner" (vv. 11-12). The harlot is always out stirring up trouble.

Solomon continues the scenario in verses 13-23: "She caught him, and kissed him, and with an impudent face said unto him, I have peace offerings with me; this day have I paid my vows. Therefore came I forth to meet thee, diligently to seek thy face, and I have found thee. I have decked my bed with coverings of tapestry, with embroidered works, with fine linen of Egypt. I have perfumed my bed with myrrh, aloes, and cinnamon. Come, let us take our fill of love until the morning; let us solace ourselves with love. For my husband is not at home; he is gone on a long journey. He hath taken a bag of money with him, and will come home at the day appointed. With her much fair speech she caused him to yield; with the flattering of her lips she forced him. He goeth after her straightway, as an ox goeth to the slaughter, or as a fool to the correction of the stocks, till an arrow strike through his liver—as a bird hasteneth to the snare, and knoweth not that it is for his life." A Christian who involves himself in sexual sin will destroy his own life.

3. Proverbs 9:17-18—Solomon cites a lewd woman as say-

ing, "Stolen waters are sweet, and bread eaten in secret is pleasant" and observes that "her guests are in the depths of sheol." There is a certain adventure in adultery, but the end result is absolutely devastating.

4. 1 Corinthians 10:8—Paul said, "Neither let us commit fornication, as some of them committed, and fell in one day three and twenty thousand." In one day, 23,000 Israelites died for committing adultery.

5. Psalm 51:2-3—David prayed, "Wash me thoroughly from mine iniquity, and cleanse me from my sin. For I acknowledge my transgressions, and my sin is ever before me." God forgave David for committing adultery with Bathsheba, but David was absolutely devastated because of his sin. He paid for that sin every waking day for the rest of his life. It destroyed his family and left him lonely. Sexual sin has a way of making you lonely. It immediately isolates you because you're afraid someone might find out. David was physically sick and had a guilty conscience that created havoc in him the rest of his life (Ps. 31:9-10). God forgave his sin, but it didn't change the consequences. David still paid a high price.

II. SEXUAL SIN CONTROLS THE BODY (v. 12b)

"All things are lawful unto me, but I will not be brought under the power of any."

A. The Enslavement of Sexual Sin

The phrase "be brought under the power of" is the Greek word *exousiasthēsomai*, which means "to come under the domination of" or "to come under the power of." It literally means "to enslave." Paul is saying in verse 12, "I will not be enslaved to sexual sin." There is no more enslaving evil than sexual sin. People who bind themselves to sexual sin are always looking for full gratification, which they never find.

B. The Ending of Sexual Sin

The Corinthian Christians were becoming slaves to sexual sin under the guise of liberty. What they did not realize was that they were actually losing their freedom in Christ. In the name of Christian freedom, they had actually become slaves to their own desires.

1. 1 Thessalonians 4:3-4—Paul said, "This is the will of God, even your sanctification, that ye should abstain from

fornication; that every one of you should know how to possess his vessel in sanctification and honor." Many interpreters say that "vessel" is a synonym for one's own body rather than for his wife's. Every believer is to rightly control his own body.

2. Romans 8:13—Paul said, "If ye live after the flesh, ye shall die; but if ye, through the Spirit, do mortify the deeds of the body, ye shall live." Paul is saying, "Gain control of your body; master the flesh." Many young people ask me, "How far should you go in a dating relationship?" I respond by saying, "You should never go further than the point at which you lose control." Someone might say, "I'm always in control." If you have that kind of attitude, you had better be careful because you can get to the place where you are victimized by your passion.

3. 1 Corinthians 9:26-27—Paul also said, "[I fight] not as one that beateth the air; but I keep under my body, and bring into subjection, lest that by any means, when I have preached to others, I myself should be a castaway." In verse 27, the phrase "keep under" is the Greek word *hupōpiazō*, which means "to give a black eye to" or "to beat the face black and blue." Paul in effect is saying, "I have to beat my body into subjection because even as a preacher I could become a castaway." Many people who name the name of Christ are castaways. Some have even preached about Christ, but because they didn't give their body a black eye—discipline themselves—their lusts ran away with them, and they sinned, becoming useless to God. Sexual sin is a driving, compelling, dominating passion in which men are taken captive.

C. The Escalation of Sexual Sin

1. Psalm 1:1—The psalmist said, "Blessed is the man who walketh not in the counsel of the ungodly, nor standeth in the way of sinners, nor sitteth in the seat of the scornful." All sin has a progressive element. First, a man is walking, then standing, and finally, sitting. No sin is more progressive and enslaving than sexual sin. The more one indulges in it, the more one is controlled. Often it begins with small indiscretions, which lead to greater ones and finally to flagrant vice.

2. James 1:13-15—James said, "Let no man say when he is tempted, I am tempted of God; for God cannot be

tempted with evil, neither tempteth he any man; but every man is tempted, when he is drawn away of his own lust, and enticed. Then when lust hath conceived, it bringeth forth sin; and sin, when it is finished, bringeth forth death." Sin, if it is dwelled upon, will be a continual battle.

3. 2 Timothy 3:13—Paul said, "Evil men and seducers shall become worse and worse, deceiving, and being deceived." The progressive element of sin is inevitable.

The Corinthians were no strangers to sexual sin, and unfortunately many believers indulged also. In the name of Christian freedom, they had become controlled by their own fleshly desires. Paul in effect says in verse 12, "Yes, all things are lawful, but if you involve yourself in sexual sin, you will become a slave to it."

III. SEXUAL SIN PERVERTS THE BODY (vv. 13-20)

"Foods for the body, and the body for foods; but God shall destroy both it and them. Now the body is not for fornication, but for the Lord; and the Lord for the body. And God hath both raised up the Lord, and will also raise up us by his own power. Know ye not that your bodies are the members of Christ? Shall I, then, take the members of Christ, and make them the members of an harlot? God forbid. What? Know ye not that he who is joined to an harlot is one body? For two, saith he, shall be one flesh. But he that is joined unto the Lord is one spirit. Flee fornication. Every sin that a man doeth is outside the body; but he that committeth fornication sinneth against his own body. What? Know ye not that your body is the temple of the Holy Spirit who is in you, whom ye have of God, and ye are not your own? For ye are bought with a price; therefore, glorify God in your body and in your spirit, which are God's."

A. The Body Is for the Lord (vv. 13-14)

1. The biological function

Food and the belly were created by God for each other (v. 13). Their relationship is purely biological. It is likely the Corinthians were using that truth as an analogy to justify their sexual immorality. Perhaps it was a popular proverb celebrating the idea that sex is no different from eating; the stomach was made for food, and the body was made for sex. But Paul stopped them short by in effect saying, "It is true that food and the stomach

15

were made for each other, but it is also true that they are merely temporal." One day, God is going to destroy both food and stomachs. The biological process of eating will have no place in the eternal state. The body is not for sexual sin, but is for the Lord, and the Lord is for the body. Why? Because God has raised up the Lord and will also raise up our bodies by His power (v. 14).

2. The spiritual union

Someday your body will be resurrected. It isn't just a temporal commodity. Our bodies will be brought out of the grave to be glorified and transformed into heavenly bodies. Don't think that the biology of eating is equal to what you do with your body, because in terms of the body's union with Christ, there is a big difference. Eating is a biological function, but sex is far more. It is a spiritual union that transcends the biological. C. S. Lewis said in *The Screwtape Letters*, "Wherever a man lies with a woman, there, whether they like it or not, a transcendental relation is set up between them which must be eternally enjoyed or eternally endured" ([New York: Macmillan, 1959], p. 83). The Bible never says God will destroy the body eternally. The body of a Christian will spend eternity with Jesus Christ in a glorified state. Our bodies have biological functions, but they are far beyond the temporal state of food and stomach. There is only a temporal reality between the food and the stomach, but between your body and the Lord, there is an eternal relationship that must not be defiled, because God wants you presented to Jesus Christ as a chaste virgin (2 Cor. 11:2). Your stomach was made for food, but your body wasn't made for sex—it was made for God. And within God's will, sex is included only in marriage. Don't defile your body, which is designed to spend eternity with Him; the body is for the Lord.

B. The Body Is a Member of Christ (vv. 15-18)

1. The extent of sexual sin

Our bodies are not only for the Lord in the future, but they are also a part of Christ's own body right now. The fact that members of Christ's own body would commit sexual sin and make themselves members with a prostitute was an incomprehensible thought to Paul. He uses the strongest negative in the Greek language, *Mē genoito*, "God forbid" or "May it never happen!" When you were saved, you were joined to Christ. Every Christian is a member of Christ's body. Christ is "head over all things to the church, which is his body, the fullness of him who filleth all in all" (Eph. 1:22-23; cf. 1 Cor. 12:12; Rom. 12:5). If a Christian commits acts of sexual sin, he is joining Christ to that act. It is unthinkable to join Jesus Christ and sexual sin together in a relationship. Committing sexual sin is like saying, "Lord, I am going over here to commit adultery; would You please come and join me?" That's blasphemous, but it's no more blasphemous than a Christian committing adultery, because he's actually making Christ partake in a reprehensible act as a member of the body of Christ.

2. The evil of sexual sin

Sex is a union of two people becoming one flesh (Gen. 2:24). Thus, if a Christian engages in sexual sin, he is making Christ one with that sin. Sex is not just biological but also spiritual in that two people become one flesh. That is the way God designed it. That is why the Old Testament admonishes two single people to marry if they engage in sexual sin, because they have consummated a spiritual union. That is why the Bible says adultery is grounds for divorce, because there has been a union consummated outside the marriage.

When you unite with a prostitute, you become one flesh with her in the deepest sense of communion within your being (v. 16). When a Christian commits adultery or when a single person is involved in sexual sin, they have been drawn into a union with that person. And you have drawn Jesus Christ into that union also. Christ is not personally tainted with that sin, but His reputation is dirtied because of the association. Verse 17 says, "He that is joined unto the Lord is one spirit." A Christian is one with Christ.

3. The erasing of sexual sin

Paul says in verse 18, "Flee fornication." The best way to handle sexual temptation is to run from it. You can't have a problem with sexual sin if you are not around it.

a) Genesis 39:12—Potiphar's wife "caught him [Joseph] by his garment, saying, Lie with me: and he left his garment in her hand, and fled, and got out." Joseph was an intelligent man. He was in a potentially com-

17

promising situation, and he got out right away. Don't say to yourself, "I'm going to stay in this tempting situation and gain the victory." That is ridiculous! If you are tempted in any way, get out of the situation.

b) 2 Timothy 2:22—Paul said, "Flee also youthful lusts." If you're looking at something that could cause you to sin, stop looking. If you are in a situation that has the potential for compromising your testimony for Christ, flee that temptation. It does not matter if people don't understand your actions; flee before you are drawn into sexual sin. When we are in danger of such immorality, we should not argue, debate, or explain, and we certainly should not try to rationalize. We are not to consider it a spiritual challenge to be met but a spiritual trap to be escaped. We should get away as fast as we can.

4. The examination of sexual sin

Paul further states in verse 18, "Every sin that a man doeth is outside the body; but he that committeth fornication sinneth against his own body." Paul does not elucidate on what he means by this statement but I believe he is saying that although sexual sin is not necessarily the worst sin, it is the most unique in its character. It rises from within the body and is bent on personal gratification. It drives like no other impulse and when fulfilled, affects the body like no other sin. It has the potential of destroying a person like no other sin. Because sexual intimacy is the deepest uniting of two persons, its abuse corrupts on the deepest level. Sexual immorality is far more destructive than alcohol, drugs, or crime. Sexual sin is the deepest penetrating sin that a person can commit because it units him to another person in the vileness of their sin.

Some years ago a sixteen-year-old girl came to my office in complete despair. She had committed so many sexual sins that she felt utterly worthless. She had not looked in a mirror for months because she could not stand to look at herself. To me she looked nearer forty than sixteen. She was on the verge of suicide, not wanting to live another day. I had the special joy in leading her to Christ and seeing the transformation He made in her life. She said, "For the first time in years, I feel clean." Sexual sin destroys a person because it diametrically opposes everything God intended for the body of a Christian.

C. The Body Is a Temple of the Holy Spirit (vv. 19-20)

Paul goes on to say in verse 19, "What? Know ye not that your body is the temple of the Holy Spirit who is in you, whom ye have of God, and ye are not your own?" As Christians, the Corinthians didn't seek or earn the Holy Spirit; He was given as a gift. The Christian's body is the actual temple or dwelling place of the Holy Spirit.

1. 1 Peter 1:18-19—Peter said, "Ye were not redeemed with corruptible things, like silver and gold, from your vain manner of life received by tradition from your fathers, but with the precious blood of Christ, as of a lamb without blemish and without spot." As Paul says in 1 Corinthians 6:20, "Ye are bought with a price." And what was that price? The blood of the Lord Jesus Christ. Paul calls for sexual purity not only because of the way sexual sin affects the body but also because the body it affects is not even the believer's own.

2. 2 Corinthians 6:16—Paul said, "What agreement hath the temple of God with idols? For ye are the temple of the living God; as God hath said, I will dwell in them, and walk in them; and I will be their God, and they shall be my people." Christians are the shrine of the Holy Spirit. And if that is so, how can a person draw the Holy Spirit into sexual sin?

The bodies of believers are God's temple, and a temple is for worship. Our bodies, therefore, have one supreme purpose: to glorify God (v. 20). The rest of the verse reads, "And in your spirit, which are God's." This addition does not appear in the best manuscripts, so the verse should end without it. Verse 20 is calling believers to live in a way that brings honor to God, who alone is worthy of our obedience and adoration.

Are you defiling the temple of the Holy Spirit by engaging in sexual sin? Are you justifying your actions by saying sex is only a biological function? If you are, the Word of God commands you to stop immediately. Your body is for the Lord. As Paul told the Ephesians, "Fornication, and all uncleanness, or covetousness, let it not be once named among you, as becometh saints" (5:3).

Focusing on the Facts

1. True or false: The church at Corinth had rationalized their sexual activity to the point that they felt they could sin without consequence (see p. 8).
2. Describe the background of the city of Corinth (see p. 8).
3. Give four reasons for Paul writing to the Corinthians (see p. 9).
4. Sexual sin _____ the body (v. 12; see p. 9).
5. What sin produces more pitfalls than any other? Explain your answer (see p.10).
6. What is the effect of sexual sin based on Proverbs 5:3-6 (see p. 10)?
7. What is God's attitude toward sex within marriage (see pp. 10-11)?
8. How can a Christian begin to eliminate sexual sin in his life? Explain your answer using Solomon's advice (see pp. 11-12).
9. Sexual sin _____ the body (v. 12; see p. 13).
10. The text gives several passages stating God's attitude toward sexual sin. What are they and what is their significance (see pp. 13-14)?
11. Describe in your own words the enslaving and progressive elements of sexual sin (see pp. 13-14).
12. Sexual sin _____ the body (v. 13-20; see p. 15).
13. Discuss the point verses 13-14 are making in regard to sex and the biological function of the body (see pp. 15-16).
14. What will ultimately happen to your body as a believer (see p. 16)?
15. True or false: If a Christian commits acts of sexual sin, he is joining Christ to that act (see p. 17).
16. What is the best way to handle sexual temptation (see p. 17)?
17. Discuss the implications of the Christian's body being the temple of the Holy Spirit (see p. 19).

Pondering the Principles

1. In 1 Corinthians 6:12 Paul expands the meaning of Christian liberty by saying, "All things are lawful unto me, but all things are not expedient." He was essentially saying, "God will forgive the believer's sin, but the price is high." Sexual sin is a unique kind of sin in that it harms the believer's own body. It entices and enslaves the person who involves himself in it. It is every Christian's responsibility to eliminate all forms of sexual immorality in his life. Are you presently involved in sexual immorality? Are you using your body for any other reason than the glory of

God? If you are, memorize 1 Thessalonians 4:3-4 and ask God to make His will a part of your life.

2. Paul says in 1 Corinthians 6:13-20 that the believer's body is for the Lord, is a member of Christ's body, and is the temple of the Holy Spirit. Are you defiling the temple of the Holy Spirit by engaging in sexual sin? Are you justifying your actions by saying it is only a biological function? If you are, the Word of God commands you to stop immediately. The next time you are tempted to sin sexually, run—literally, if need be—from that temptation (Gen. 39:1-15). God will give you grace to handle any temptation if you are willing to say no to sexual sin (1 Cor. 10:13). Ask God right now to help you flee from sexual sin.

2
To Marry or Not to Marry

Outline

Introduction
A. Jesus' Teaching on Marriage
   1. Marriage is designed by God
   2. Marriage is to be monogamous
   3. Marriage is to be unbroken
   4. Marriage is only for this life
B. Paul's Teaching on Marriage
   1. Morality in Corinth
   2. Marriages in the Roman Empire
     a) The confusion over definition
       (1) *Contubernium*
       (2) *Usus*
       (3) *Coemptio in manum*
       (4) *Confarreatio*
     b) The chaos causing divorce
       (1) Homosexuality
       (2) Polygamy
       (3) The use of concubines
       (4) The women's liberation movement

Lesson
A. The Question of Celibacy
B. The Question of Marriage
I. Celibacy Is Good (v. 1)
  A. Genesis 20:6
  B. Ruth 2:9
  C. Proverbs 6:29
    1. Paul's instruction
    2. Jewish insistence
II. Celibacy Is Tempting (v. 2)
  A. The Danger of Celibacy

Introduction

The Bible has a lot to say about marriage in the New Testament. The Lord Jesus taught about it many times in the gospel records.

    A. Jesus' Teaching on Marriage

      1. Marriage is designed by God

Jesus says in Matthew 19:4-6, "Have ye not read that he who made them at the beginning, made them male and female; and said, For this cause shall a man leave father and mother, and shall cleave to his wife, and they two shall be one flesh? Wherefore, they are no more two, but one flesh. What, therefore, God hath joined together, let no man put asunder." God specifically designed man and woman for each other. He stated that in marriage God Himself actually joins two people together.

      2. Marriage is to be monogamous

Jesus also emphasized that marriage is to be monogamous, or that it is to be a one-man one-woman relationship. In Mark 10:6-9 Jesus is simply reiterating what God had already declared in Genesis 2:24: "From the beginning of the creation God made them male and female. For this cause shall a man leave his father and mother, and cleave to his wife; and they two shall be one flesh; so then they are no more two, but one flesh. What, therefore, God hath joined together, let not man put asunder."

3. Marriage is to be unbroken

Jesus teaches in Matthew 5:31-32 that marriage is to be unbroken. He said, "It hath been said, Whosoever shall put away his wife, let him give her a writing of divorcement; but I say unto you that whosoever shall put away his wife, except for the cause of fornication, causeth her to commit adultery; and whosoever shall marry her that is divorced committeth adultery." God hasn't changed His attitude at all about divorce.

4. Marriage is only for this life

Jesus also taught that marriage is only for this life. In Matthew 22:30 He says, "In the resurrection they [human beings] neither marry, nor are given in marriage, but are like the angels of God in heaven" (cf. Mark 12:25; Luke 20:35). These passages all indicate that marriage is only for this earth and not for heaven.

Even though the Lord had much to say about marriage, He covered only the basic theological issues surrounding it. He identified the institution of marriage without dealing with the practical applications of it. He later gave revelation through His apostles so that when we read the epistles, we find much more information about the practical application of marriage. The apostle Paul particularly had much to say about the subject of marriage from various angles.

Paul's Writings—Opinion or Inspiration?

Unfortunately many people discard some of Paul's writings as illegitimate parts of the Bible. For instance, they want to dismiss 1 Corinthians 7 because Paul puts supposed disclaimers throughout the chapter, trying to tell us that what he says is simply his opinion. They point to 1 Corinthians 7:12, where Paul says, "But to the rest speak I, not the Lord." They say, "He wants to make it clear that this is his opinion, not God's."

They will also point to 1 Corinthians 7:25, where Paul says, "Now concerning virgins, I have no commandment of the Lord." Paul also says, "She is happier if she so abide, after my judgment; and I think also that I have the Spirit of God" (v. 40). The critics say Paul didn't know whether he had God's perspective or not and assume his is a rather hopeless attempt at mixing opinion with revelation. They claim the best thing to do is discard it. That is an inaccurate view, however, if Paul's statements are seen in another light.

It is true that Paul nowhere in his other epistles gives statements such as these, but that does not mean he is simply giving his own opinion. The reason he makes those statements is that he is speaking new truth. He is not quoting something spoken about by Jesus in the gospels. When Paul reaches back, interfacing with what the Lord taught, he says, "Look, I'm going to tell you something about being married that isn't just from me; the Lord already said it." Then in verse 12 he says, "But to the rest speak I, not the Lord." In other words, he says, "This is something new that the Lord didn't talk about. I'm no longer quoting the Lord." In verse 10 it's as if Paul, when quoting Jesus, says, "Quote . . . end quote." But in verse 12, he is giving new instructions that are not covered in Christ's words. Paul is not disclaiming inspiration; his revelation is on an equal plane with the Lord's.

That is why I don't like red-letter editions of the Bible. They imply that what Jesus said is more important than what any other biblical writer said. So is what Paul said equally as important as what the Lord said? Yes; what Jesus said and what Paul said both came from God. There are no degrees of inspiration. The entire Bible is the revelation of the Spirit of God. It's all right if you have a red-letter Bible, as long as you realize that the verses in red are not more important than any other verses. When our Lord is giving the parables of the kingdom in Matthew 13, He says the disciples are scribes. That meant the disciples were going to be the writers of the New Testament. He says in verse 52, "Every scribe who is instructed concerning the kingdom of heaven is like a man that is an householder, who bringeth forth out of his treasure things new and old." Jesus was explaining that the disciples were being trained by Him to dispense old and new truth, just as Paul is doing here in 1 Corinthians 7. Paul is bringing new truth to light, given to him by the Lord Jesus Christ Himself.

B. Paul's Teaching on Marriage

First Corinthians 7-11 comprise Paul's authoritative answers to the Corinthian believers' practical questions (7:1). The letter was probably delivered by Stephanas, Fortunatus, and Achaicus (16:17). The Corinthians were asking questions in four major areas: marriage (chap. 7), meat offered to idols (chaps. 8-10), women (11:2-16), and the Lord's Table (11:17-34).

1. Morality in Corinth

   Marriage was an area in which the Corinthians had serious problems. To understand the context of Paul's writing, we have to know something of the problems the Corinthians would face as new believers in the area of marriage. They were having problems adjusting to their new life in the church and the community.

2. Marriages in the Roman Empire

   Much of the Corinthian's marital trouble reflected the pagan and morally corrupt society in which they lived and from which they had not fully separated themselves. The Roman Empire had no uniform set of marital laws. You could get married at least four different ways in the Roman Empire, all of which were recognized in some sense. Much of the population of the Roman world were slaves, maybe as many as several million. These slaves weren't even considered human beings and therefore had none of the rights of citizens. In a strict sense, marriage didn't exist for slaves, because they were treated like animals. A farmer wouldn't marry his cows or goats; he mated them. In the same way they didn't marry slaves—they mated them.

   a) The confusion over definition

      The four different kinds of marriages in the Roman Empire were:

      (1) *Contubernium*

          When two slaves wanted to get married, rather than having an official marriage, the owner of the slaves would agree to what was called a *contubernium*, which simply means "tent companionship." The owner would allow them to live in a tent together, and that constituted a certain kind of marriage. If the owner didn't like the marriage relationship, he could separate them or sell off one or the other. That created problems in the early church because many of the early Christians were slaves and would have had mixed-up marital backgrounds.

          The Corinthian believers were wondering if they were supposed to end their marriages once they had come to Christ. Paul said no. He emphasized the sanctity of the marriage, regardless of its legal basis. Even to those simply living together under a tent companionship, he was saying, "Stay together; prove yourselves true to one another. Love one another and make of your marriage what God designed it to be."

(2) *Usus*

When we move one step beyond the slaves, we come to the marriage of the common people in the Roman culture. They were married under the custom called *usus*. Today we would call it common-law marriage. This particular custom meant that a man and woman could live together for one year, and at the end of that year, they would become identified as husband and wife.

The church would have had to deal with people who had no legal paper to identify their marriage. The Lord Jesus didn't discuss that particular issue, so Paul had to instruct the Corinthians on the sanctity of marriage.

(3) *Coemptio in manum*

The third form of marriage was marriage by sale. A father could sell his daughter to the highest bidder, who then became her husband. If the bidder could come up with the right price, the girl was his. If the father had a lousy business but a beautiful daughter, he could bail out his business by selling his daughter to the highest bidder.

(4) *Confarreatio*

The most noble families of the Roman Empire had a sophisticated marriage ceremony called *confarreatio*. It involved exchanging rings and placing them on what we call the ring finger of the left hand. This custom came from the second century Roman writer Aulus Gellius, who taught that there is a nerve running from that finger to the heart (*Gellius* 10.10). They also had a cake, wore veils, had music, held hands, and had wreaths. Our modern-day marriage ceremonies are directly related to these pagan ceremonies.

The church at Corinth was filled with people who were married in each of those four ways (although it is possible that *usus* may have been banned by this time). They were fraught with many questions about their future. They had been so accustomed to the Roman culture that they didn't know how to respond. The apostle Paul wasn't about to impose laws on the Roman Empire. He and the other New Testament writers and teachers simply taught the sanctity of marriage, encouraging the new converts to make the most of their situation.

b) The chaos causing divorce

To add to the Corinthian problem, divorce was rampant. Commentator William Barclay noted one historical document describing a lady who was getting married for the twenty-seventh time, and she was going to be the twenty-sixth wife of her husband-to-be! Many counted their years by their wives. Several factors contributed to the high divorce rate. Among them were:

(1) Homosexuality

(2) Polygamy

(3) The use of concubines

Seneca said that men used their wives to clean up the house and cook the meals while they used concubines for physical pleasure (cited in J. Plassard's *Le concubinat romain sous le Haut Empire*).

(4) The women's liberation movement

Jerome Carcopino in his book *Daily Life in Ancient Rome* (New Haven: Yale, 1940) writes, "Alongside the heroines of the imperial aristocracy, the irreproachable wives and the excellent mothers who were still found within its ranks, it is easy to sight "emancipated," or rather "unbridled," wives, who . . . evaded the duties of maternity for fear of losing their good looks; some took a pride in being behind their husbands in no sphere of activity, and vied with them in tests of strength which their sex would have seemed to forbid; some were not content to live their lives by their husband's side, but carried on another life without him. . . . Whether because of voluntary birth control, or because of the impoverishment of the stock, many Roman marriages at the end of the first and the beginning of the second

29

century were childless" (p. 90). Carcopino points out that according to the sixth satire of first century Roman writer Juvenal, "women were quitting their embroidery, stopping their reading, and stopping their songs to put their efforts into competing with men." Juvenal asks, "What modesty can you expect in a woman who wears a helmet, abjures her own sex, and delights in feats of strength?" (p. 92). Juvenal is also quoted as saying that women joined men's hunting parties, and with spear in hand and breasts exposed, took to pig-sticking.

Before long, marriages began to suffer. Vows were violated. Women demanded to live their own lives. And as soon as the women wanted out, the husbands could take no more and began to discard their women for going out without a veil, speaking to the wrong person in public, or going somewhere without asking their permission. They would even divorce a woman to get a richer one, as in the case of the Roman orator Cicero.

Not only did men discard women, but women began to shed their husbands as well. Juvenal wrote: "Thus does she lord it over her husband. But before long she vacates her kingdom; she flits from one home to another wearing out her bridal veil" (p. 99).

The picture of a right marriage could be a confusing issue. People were in and out of marriages; divorce was rampant. There were problems about who was really married and who wasn't. There were problems with those who were in tent companionships. If his master sold his wife, was a slave free to remarry? The Corinthians had problems that desperately needed resolving.

Lesson

A. The Question of Celibacy

In the midst of all those problems, many Corinthian Christians suggested that the best way to handle all their problems was to never get married. They began to elevate celibacy as the spiritual thing to do. Some Corinthian believers had the notion that being single and celibate was more spiritual than being married, and they began to disparage marriage entirely.

If you were single and celibate, you were considered part of the spiritual elite. You had supposedly denied the flesh and laid aside all in order to totally devote yourself to Jesus Christ. There was a prevailing view in the Corinthian church that celibacy was the highest form of the Christian life. People even began condemning those who were married. Those who were married were leaving their partners to become celibate so they could be more spiritual. People who were married to unbelievers were divorcing their spouses because they were being taught that marriage to an unbeliever was defiling.

B. The Question of Marriage

The Jewish leaders, on the other hand, were pressuring people to marry because they thought it was a sin not to be married. The situation in Corinth was difficult and perplexing, even for mature Christians. The Corinthians had many questions, so they wrote Paul and asked him to help them with the problem of marriage. The questions were numerous: What do we do now that we are believers? Should we stay together as husband and wife if we are both Christians? Should we get divorced if our spouse is an unbeliever? Should we become or remain single? The chaos of marital possibilities posed myriad perplexities, which Paul approaches in this section of his epistle.

I. CELIBACY IS GOOD (v. 1)

"Now concerning the things about which ye wrote unto me, it is good for a man not to touch a woman."

The phrase "to touch a woman" was a common Jewish euphemism for sexual intercourse. It can be easily explained by looking at some Old Testament passages.

A. Genesis 20:6—"God said unto him [Abimelech] in a dream, Yea, I know that thou didst this in the integrity of thy heart; for I also withheld thee from sinning against me: therefore allowed I thee not to touch her." Here was a case where adultery could have been committed within the family of Abraham. But God did not allow Abimelech to "touch" or to have a sexual relationship with Sarah.

B. Ruth 2:9—Boaz said, "Let thine eyes be on the field that they do reap, and go thou after them. Have I not charged the

31

young men that they shall not touch thee?" Boaz had a desire to keep Ruth pure.

C. Proverbs 6:29—"So he that goeth in to his neighbor's wife; whosoever toucheth her shall not be innocent."

1. Paul's instruction

Verse 1 is talking about a sexual relationship. Paul is saying it is good thing for Christians not to be involved in a sexual relationship—that it is good to be single. He does not say, however, that singleness is the only good condition or that marriage is in any way wrong or inferior to singleness.

Many people today think there is something wrong with you if you remain single. They say, "Well, she's not married. There must be something wrong." But Paul affirms that it is a good thing not to be married. He does not say it is better to be single; he simply says it is beneficial or profitable (Gk., *kalos*).

2. Jewish insistence

Paul responded that way because the Jews in the church were teaching that if you didn't have a wife, you were a sinner. They would say that a man who does not have a wife and child has slain his posterity and lessened the image of God in the world. According to the Jewish leaders there were seven kinds of people who couldn't get to heaven, and number one was a Jew who had no wife. The second was a wife who had no children. They theorized that since God said to be fruitful and multiply (Gen. 1:28), you were being disobedient if you remained single.

God did declare at creation that "it is not good that the man should be alone; I will make him an help fit for him" (Gen. 2:18). It is true that all people need companionship, but you can also be single and still not be alone. You can have friends. Psalm 68:6 says: "God setteth the solitary in families." God will give you someone to fulfill your need for companionship. Paul acknowledges that singleness is good, honorable, and excellent, but he does not support the claim that it is a more spiritual state or that it is more acceptable to God than marriage.

II. CELIBACY IS TEMPTING (v. 2)

"Nevertheless, to avoid fornication, let every man have his own wife, and let every woman have her own husband."

"Celibacy may be a good thing," Paul says, "but for most people it's pretty tempting. So if your celibacy is going to cause you to sin sexually, then you ought to marry." The usual complaint of the single person is that singleness is difficult, so Paul says if you are going to battle an innate desire for marriage, you may be called of God to be married.

A. The Danger of Celibacy

Paul was not implying that every believer in the Corinthian church was immoral, although many of them were. He is speaking of the danger of fornication for those who were single. Because sexual desire is unfulfilled and can be strong, there is great temptation to sexual immorality for those who are not married, especially in societies—such as that of ancient Rome and our own—where sexual looseness is freely practiced and even glorified. The gross life-style of Corinth made it harder for the unmarried to remain pure. Many unmarried people today have problems because of the constant barrage of sexual temptation.

B. The Desirability of Marriage

When speaking about the danger of celibacy, Paul is not downgrading the institution of marriage. Marriage cannot be reduced simply to being God's escape valve for the sex drive. He is not suggesting that Christians go out and find another Christian to marry only to keep from getting into moral sin. He is saying it is the normal thing to get married because it is normal to have physical desire.

Six Reasons for Marriage
Some people say Paul had a low view of marriage, but he was simply acknowledging the reality of the sexual temptations of singleness. He was stressing that the Corinthians had a legitimate outlet in marriage. The Scriptures give numerous reasons for marriage.

1. Procreation

In Genesis 1:28 God brings a man and a woman together, marries them, and tells them to be fruitful and fill the earth. One of the primary reasons for marriage is God's desire for believers to reproduce godly people. Psalm 127:3-5 says, "Lo, children are an heritage from the Lord; and the fruit of the womb is his reward. As arrows are in the hand of a mighty man, so are children of one's youth. Happy is the man who hath his quiver full of them." God created marriage for procreation.

2. Pleasure

   Marriage is also for pleasure. Hebrews 13:4 says, "Marriage is honorable in all, and the bed undefiled." Marriage was designed by God to be an honorable and enjoyable experience. First Corinthians 7:4 says that the husband's body is his wife's and that the wife's body is her husband's. They each belong to the other. The Old Testament also talks about the satisfaction and pleasure of the physical relationship of marriage (e.g. Prov. 5:18-19; Song of Solomon).

3. Provision

   God wants a man to provide what a woman needs. First Peter 3:7 says, "Ye husbands, dwell with them according to knowledge, giving honor unto the wife, as unto the weaker vessel." God knows that a man can be a strength to his wife's weaknesses. Ephesians 5:25-33 says that the husband is to provide and care for his wife, being a savior in a sense.

4. Partnership

   Marriage is also for partnership. When God made Eve, He said He made for Adam a helper—someone to come alongside. In marriage, you don't do things alone; you do them together. In our spouse, God gives us a good friend—and friendship is a key ingredient in marriage.

5. Picture

   According to Ephesians 5:22-33, marriage is a picture of Christ's relationship to His church. It is a graphic demonstration in the face of the world that God has an ongoing, unending relationship with the bride whom He loves and for whom He died.

6. Purity

   Marriage is also designed by God to keep us from committing fornication. In 1 Corinthians 7:2 Paul says, "Nevertheless, to avoid fornication, let every man have his own wife." (The word *own* prohibits polygamy.) Marriage is designed for the purity of believers.

   Although celibacy is good, it is not superior to marriage, and it has dangers and temptations that marriage does not have.

III. CELIBACY IS WRONG FOR MARRIED PEOPLE (vv. 3-5)

"Let the husband render unto the wife her due; and likewise also, the wife unto the husband. The wife hath not power of her own body, but the husband; and likewise also the husband hath not power of his own body, but the wife. Defraud ye not one the other, except it be with consent for a time, that ye may give yourselves to fasting and prayer; and come together again, that Satan tempt you not for your incontinency."

A. The Obligation in Marriage (v. 3)

The fact that celibacy is wrong for those who are married should be an obvious truth, but it was not obvious to some of the Corinthian believers. There is no place for celibacy in marriage. The word *due* is literally "the debt" and refers to an obligation. Paul is saying that when you get married, you become obligated to meet the physical needs of your partner.

Some overzealous husbands apparently had decided to set themselves apart for God. In doing so, however, they neglected or even denied their responsibilities to their wives, especially in the area of sexual relations. Some wives had done the same thing. Paul is emphasizing that married believers are not to sexually deprive their spouses, whether the spouse is a Christian or not.

Verse 3 is in the present imperative in the Greek text and literally says, "Let the husband continually keep on rendering to his wife the debt and likewise also the wife keep on rendering the debt she owes her husband." The sexual relationship in marriage is to be a continual giving to one another. There must be a growing intimacy of two lives, blended together in all dimensions, into an unbreakable bond of love. God made sexual satisfaction a great part of marriage. He holds all marriage to be sacred, and holds sexual relations between husband and wife not only to be sacred but also proper and even obligatory. God makes it clear that physical relations within marriage are not simply a privilege and a pleasure but a responsibility. Your physical union in marriage can be expressed in any way you desire. That is God's design. The Bible glorifies sexuality in marriage. The Song of Solomon is a book written solely about the physical aspect of marriage. God designed marriage to be a physical expression of love. He honors sexual desire in marriage.

The sexual act itself strengthens love in marriage. In his book *Sex and Sanity*, Stuart Babbage says, "From one point of view

35

it may be spoken of as a safety valve for irresistible desire, but, for the Christian man, it is infinitely more than that—a breathtaking experience (in Barth's words), 'a bold and blessed intoxication'. . . . Intercourse is not only the appropriate means for the expression of love, it is also the means by which love itself is strengthened and sustained. Sexual intercourse is far more than a physical act" ([London: Hodder and Stoughton, 1965], p. 37).

B. The Obedience in Marriage (v. 4)

Paul says, "The wife hath not power of her own body, but the husband and likewise also, the husband hath not power of his own body but the wife." Two imperative commands in verses 2-3 are followed by two indicatives in verse 4 stating facts. According to this verse, you give up the right to your body—it belongs to your partner. You have released the authority over your own body to your partner.

The present tense of *exousia*, which means "to have authority over," indicates a general statement that is always true. This mutual authority over one another's bodies is continuous; it lasts throughout the marriage. Now, a Christian's body is his own to take care of and use as a gift from God. And in the deepest spiritual sense, it belongs entirely to God (Rom. 12:1). But in a marital situation, it also belongs to the marriage partner. Paul is saying, "Don't break up the sexuality in your marriage just because you have become a Christian."

It isn't more spiritual to be celibate. It is good to be single, but it is great to be married, if that's God's will for you. Peter called marriage "the grace of life" (1 Pet. 3:7). Marriage is a permanent surrender of everything to your partner. You belong to one another in the fullest and truest sense.

C. The Occasion for Abstinence (v. 5)

1. The emphatic command

Paul gives an emphatic command in verse 5: "Defraud ye not one the other." The Corinthians were depriving each other of the physical part of the marriage relationship. Paul is saying, "Stop depriving one another." Sexual relations between man and wife are God-ordained and a divine command.

2. The exception clause

Paul gives only one exception to sexual activity in a marriage. He says, "Except it be with consent for a time, that ye may give yourselves to fasting and prayer; and come together again, that Satan tempt you not for your incontinency" (v. 5). Paul gives specific guidelines if, as a married couple, you decide not to enter into sexual activity.

a) "With consent"

First, it must be with consent; you must have a mutual agreement. The Greek word for "consent" is *sumphōnou,* which is the source of the English word *symphony,* and it means that unless your hearts are in symphony or agreement, sexual abstinence is wrong. If you force sexual withdrawal from your partner, you are robbing him or her. But if you both agree, then God will honor your decision.

b) "For a time"

Paul also says that sexual abstinence should only be "for a time." The phrase does not mean for a long time—but a set time. It does not mean indefinitely but for a specifically prescribed time.

c) "To pray"

Paul emphasizes that the reason for sexual abstinence in marriage is for a time of prayer. The term *fasting* does not occur in the better manuscripts, so it is best not to include it. It is not that fasting could not be a part of the prayer time; it's just that it isn't in the earlier, more reliable manuscripts. You are to give yourselves to a specific time and a specific need for prayer. There is a definite article in the Greek text in reference to this time of prayer, indicating a definite and specific kind of burden.

There may be times when you agree not to have any sexual activity because you want to pray, but that is an exception only. As in the case of fasting, if both partners agree to abstain for a brief period to allow one or both of them to spend time in intensive prayer, they may do so. Both the ideas of a specific period of time and a specific purpose for prayer are implied. It should be agreed upon in advance.

There may be times in your life when you fall into sin and need a time of purification where your heart needs to be refocused totally upon the Lord. If that is the case, you may need to withdraw from the physical relationship for a while to confess your sins.

(1) Exodus 19:15—"He [Moses] said unto the people, Be ready on the third day: come not near your wives." After the covenant at Sinai had been given, the Lord planned to come down and manifest Himself before the children of Israel. He wanted them to confess their sins before He visited them. They were to separate themselves physically from their spouses in preparation for that time. Moses commanded them to consecrate themselves by washing their clothes and by abstaining from sexual intercourse for three days (vv. 9-15).

(2) Joel 2:16—The Lord said, "Gather the people, sanctify the congregation, assemble the elders, gather the children, and those that nurse at the breasts; let the bridegroom go forth from his chamber, and the bride out of her room." The Assyrians were threatening to destroy Israel and in response to their wickedness, God commanded them to turn from their evil. The need for forgiveness was so great that even the bride and the bridegroom were to leave their nuptial chambers to join in national mourning and penitence.

(3) Zechariah 12:11-12—The Scripture says, "In that day [the second coming of Christ], shall there be a great mourning in Jerusalem, as the mourning of Hadadrimmon, in the Valley of Megiddon. And the land shall mourn, every family apart; the family of the house of David apart, and their wives apart; the family of the house of Nathan apart, and their wives apart." Marriage relations will be forsaken during that time of mourning.

3. The explicit concern

Paul says at the end of verse 5: "And then come together again." The reason for coming together again for sexual relations is explicit: "That Satan tempt you not for your incontinency." The word *incontinency* refers to a lack of self-control. There are people who use the sexual aspect of marriage to manipulate their spouse in achieving what they want. But when you withhold sexual intimacy from your partner for any reason, you put him in a situation where Satan could tempt him for a lack of self-control. Bitterness, anguish, and anxiety can come between husband and wife when sexual fulfillment is withheld. Evil thoughts can be entertained, which might lead to an adulterous situation. Do not deprive your marriage partner of sexual intimacy. In so doing, you become Satan's agent in potential sexual temptation. If you love your spouse, you will never willfully put him or her in a potentially tempting situation.

IV. CELIBACY IS A GIFT (vv. 6-7)

"But I speak this by permission, and not by commandment. For I would that all men were even as I myself. But every man hath his proper gift of God, one after this manner, and another after that."

A. The Allowance of Celibacy (v. 6)

The word *permission* is not a good translation in verse 6. The Greek word *suggnōme* means "to think the same as someone." It can also mean "allowance." In 2 Maccabees, an extrabiblical writing, the same word is translated, "aware" (14:31). Paul could be saying, "I'm saying what I'm saying because I am aware of your human needs but not by way of commandment." He was aware of the goodness of being single and celibate, yet also aware of the privileges and responsibilities of marriage. His comments are not to be interpreted as a command for every believer to be married. He recognized the predominance of marriage but also recognized that there were those who have been gifted by God to remain single.

Marriage was instituted by God and is the norm for society; it is a great blessing to mankind. But it is not required for believers or for anyone else. The point is, if you are single, that is good; and if you are married, stay married and retain normal marital relations, for that is of God. Spirituality is not determined by one's marital status.

B. The Advantage of Celibacy (v. 7a)

Paul says in verse 7, "I would that all men were even as I myself." There's a sense in which Paul wishes that everyone could be single and celibate, as he was. He might have been married at one time but now as a single person was encouraging those in the process of that decision to consider his situation. Paul recognized great liberty and freedom in remaining single. In verses 29-30 Paul says, "This I say, brethren, The time is short; it remaineth that both they that have wives be as though they had none; and they that weep as though they wept not; and they that rejoice, as though they rejoiced not." Paul was saying believers have to turn away from the things of this life; because the time is short, we're to focus on divine things.

While marriage is not a command, it is stressed as the norm because of the problem of purity. There are some, like Paul, who aren't married because they have a special gift of God. The next time you see a single person, don't assume that there's something wrong with him.

You might assume, first of all, that he has a gift of God and is uniquely prepared by the Holy Spirit for singleness. (This gift is different from the spiritual gifts bestowed on every believer that we read about in Romans 12, 1 Corinthians 12, and Ephesians 4). Many might say, "I couldn't stand being single!" That may mean you don't have the gift of singleness. Singleness is the gift of being single and not being consumed by lust.

C. The Appropriation of Celibacy (v. 7b)

Paul ends verse 7 by saying, "Every man hath his proper gift of God, one after this manner, and another after that." The gift of celibacy is being single and enjoying it. It is being single and not being tempted to fall into sexual sin. The gift of being single means not being preoccupied with marriage. It is understandable why Paul says what he does about the privilege of remaining single. There are some things in the ministry that a single man could do more easily than a married man.

1. A commended gift

Paul says in verse 32, "I would have you without care. He that is unmarried careth for the things that belong to the Lord, how he may please the Lord." It is easier for a single person to totally dedicate his time, energy, and talents to the work of the ministry. Paul gives a contrast in verse 33: "But he that is married careth for the things that are of the world, how he may please his wife." If you are married, you have certain things to be taken care of, including your wife and children. But if you are single, you have more freedom to serve the Lord.

Rachel Saint served as a single missionary among the Auca Indians of Ecuador for many years. She poured out her life and her love to Indians who murdered her brother and four other missionaries, and found great blessing and fulfillment. (Their story is recounted in Elisabeth Elliot's *Through Gates of Splendor* [Wheaton, Ill.: Tyndale, 1981].)

2. A commissioned gift

Jesus Himself stated that being single is a good thing. He says in Matthew 19:12, "There are some eunuchs, who were so born from their mother's womb; and there are some eunuchs, who were made eunuchs by men; and there are eunuchs, who have made themselves eunuchs for the kingdom of heaven's sake. He that is able to receive it, let him receive it." The last group of single persons Jesus mentioned decided not to marry so they could fully serve the Lord and His kingdom. And in 1 Corinthians 7, Paul further defines the ability to make that decision as a gift of the Holy Spirit.

Thank God if you're single and have no desire for marriage; use it for His glory. If you're married, enjoy it and use it for His glory. Thank God for whatever state you're in because it is His perfect and divine plan for you.

Focusing on the Facts

1. Describe Jesus' teaching on marriage (see pp. 24-25).
2. Discuss the importance of Paul's writings in 1 Corinthians 7. Explain why they are not merely the reflection of his own opinion but the product of divine inspiration (see pp. 25-26).
3. List the topics Paul discusses in 1 Corinthians 7-11 (see p. 26).
4. You could get married four different ways in the Roman Empire. Name and discuss each (see pp. 27-29).
5. Describe some of the problems causing divorce in Corinth (see p. 29).
6. How were the Corinthian Christians handling the question of celibacy (see pp. 30-31)?
7. How were the Corinthian believers being influenced by the Jewish leaders in regard to marriage (see p. 31)?
8. Explain what Paul meant by saying, "It is good for a man not to touch a woman" (see pp. 31-32).
9. What was the danger concerning celibacy in the Corinthian

church? What problems exist in the church today in this area (see p. 32)?

10. Name six reasons for marriage and explain the significance of each (see pp. 33-34).

11. What specific obligation does the spouse owe his mate (1 Cor. 7:3-4; see p. 35)?

12. God designed marriage to be a _____ expression of love (see p. 35).

13. True or false: In marriage, both partners have released authority over their own body to fulfill the sexual needs of their mate (see p. 36).

14. What three things must be present if a couple decides to abstain from sexual fulfillment (see p. 37)?

15. What are the possible results of withholding sexual fulfillment from your partner (see pp. 37-38)?

16. What are the advantages of remaining single (see pp. 39-40)?

17. Explain the purpose Jesus gave for remaining single according to Matthew 19:12 (see p. 41).

Pondering the Principles

1. Paul says in 1 Corinthians 7:1, "It is good for a man not to touch a woman." Paul instructs that celibacy is good. He does not say that singleness is the only good condition or that marriage is in any way wrong or inferior to singleness. Are you single? Do you struggle with being single? If you are, Paul is saying to you that being single is good. It is even in many ways more advantageous than being married in your service for Christ. Look at 1 Corinthians 7:1 again and thank God for your singleness. Ask Him to strengthen you for more effective service.

2. Paul also said that celibacy is tempting. To avoid fornication, most men and women need to marry to fulfill their sexual desires. Have you made a decision about remaining single? Do you struggle with sexual temptation? If you are struggling, it may be that you do not have the special gift given by God to remain single. Reread 1 Corinthians 7:1-7 and ask God to reveal His will concerning your singleness. Seek Him in all you do and He will direct your path.

3. Another principle we studied was that celibacy is wrong for married people. Paul was saying in 1 Corinthians 7:3-5 that when you do get married, you are obligated to meet the physical needs of your partner. Sexual relations between husband and wife are

God-ordained and a divine command. As a married person, are you withholding sexual fulfillment from your partner? If so, the Scriptures command you to stop depriving your partner. The first thing you need to do is to repent and confess your sin to God. Go then to your spouse and ask forgiveness. Always seek to provide for your spouse the sexual fulfillment that he or she needs.

3

Divine Guidelines for Marriage

Outline

Introduction
A. The Present Problem
B. The Past Predicament
    1. The confusion
    2. The characteristics
C. The Previous Principles
    1. Marriage is good
    2. Marriage is not for everyone

Lesson
I. Guidelines for Single Christians (vv. 8-9)
    A. The Ideal Plan
    B. The Ideal Purpose
    C. The Ideal Proposal
        1. The pressure involved
        2. The price involved
            a) Matthew 19:10-12
            b) Luke 2:36-37
        3. The problems involved
            a) Man's sinful nature
            b) Man's selfish nature
        4. The precept involved
II. Guidelines for Christians Married to Other Christians (vv. 10-11)
    A. The Lord's Command (v. 10)
    B. The Apostle's Command (v. 11)
        1. The reiteration
        2. The reinforcement
III. Guidelines for Christians Married to Unbelievers Who Want to Stay (vv. 12-14)
    A. The Questions

Introduction

A. The Present Problem

It is difficult to maintain a marriage in today's world. There are nearly as many divorces as marriages, and the statistics continue to skyrocket. Love today is loudly acclaimed and sought after but it is not often evident—even within many marriages.

B. The Past Predicament

Unfortunately, marriage problems are not a new phenomenon. Such conflict has existed throughout history. Marriage problems were rampant in New Testament times, especially in the Roman Empire.

The church in Corinth was severely afflicted with all kinds of marital conflicts. The seventh chapter of 1 Corinthians was written to answer the questions that arose as a result. The apostle Paul addressed the Corinthians' needs, misconceptions, and misbehavior.

1. The confusion

The Corinthian Christians were confused because some were saying it was better to remain single to be more spiritual. They had a growing fascination with celibacy and thought that if they remained single, they would be able to give a higher devotion to God. They assumed that would move them to a higher plain of spirituality and even went so far as to say any kind of sex was wrong. That caused many Christians to divorce their spouses for so-called "spiritual reasons" or to remain married but

46

withdraw from any physical contact to devote themselves totally to God. The Jewish leaders, on the other hand, had propagated their belief that you had to be married to be godly, and that if you weren't married, you were out of God's will and excluded from heaven.

2. The characteristics

Several questions naturally arose in the Corinthian church:

a) Is marriage a command?

b) Do you have to be married to please God?

c) Should believers marry or is it more spiritual to stay single?

d) Are you a more devoted Christian if you are not married?

e) Should married people who have subsequently come to Christ abstain from sex?

f) Should a Christian married to a non-Christian get a divorce?

C. The Previous Principles

In 1 Corinthians 7:1-7 we studied the general principles regarding marriage.

1. Marriage is good

Paul affirmed that marriage is normal. It is for the majority. God designed the institution of marriage. It is intended for those who cannot otherwise avoid sexual involvement. That does not mean you should go out and get married immediately just because you can't control your desires. Paul is saying that those who have a desire for sexual fulfillment most likely do not have the gift of singleness.

2. Marriage is not for everyone

Marriage is good, but it is not an absolute commandment for everyone to obey because God has given some the gift of being single (v. 7), which is the ability to totally control sexual desire. If you have been gifted with singleness, you have a unique gift of God that should be used for His glory. Those who have the gift of celibacy have a special blessing of God that should be maintained because it puts them in a position to be used by Him in a unique way.

47

In verses 8-16 Paul supplies answers to four different groups of people: (1) those who were formerly married (vv. 8-9); (2) those who are married to believers (vv. 10-11); (3) those who are married to unbelievers who want to remain married (vv. 12-14); and (4) those who are married to unbelievers who want to leave the marriage (vv. 15-16).

Lesson

I. GUIDELINES FOR SINGLE CHRISTIANS (vv. 8-9)

"I say, therefore, to the unmarried and widows, It is good for them if they abide even as I. But if they cannot have self-control, let them marry; for it is better to marry than to burn."

Formerly married people came to salvation in Christ and asked if they now had the right to remarry someone else. The unmarried (those divorced before coming to Christ) and especially widows desired answers to their questions because of their past situation. Widows had known all the joys of marriage but were now alone. The unmarrieds had also experienced marriage and had many questions about their future. Paul deals with each situation as the chapter unfolds.

A. The Ideal Plan

Paul's response to those who fit in this category is, "It is good for them if they abide even as I" (v. 8). Paul affirms that if you are divorced or widowed, it would be good if you remained single. The Greek word for "good" is *kalos*, which means "beneficial" or "excellent." Paul is saying, "Don't listen to Jewish leaders who are saying if you're not married you're abnormal." Before we criticize the Jewish leaders too much, we need to realize that many well meaning Christians today do the same thing. We see a young person and we tell them they should get married before it's too late. However, their singleness may be God's best for their lives.

B. The Ideal Purpose

Single people are needed in Christianity to help fulfill the plan of God. It is all right if someone has the need to marry, but if someone has no interest in marriage and feels God has given him the gift of celibacy, let him fulfill what God intends to do through his life. Paul was speaking to the unmarried, or people who were divorced before coming to Christ. They wanted to know if they had the right to marry again. His word to them was, "It is good for them if they abide even as I" (v. 8).

By that statement Paul affirms that he was formerly married. Marriage seems to have been required for membership in the Sanhedrin, to which Paul may have once belonged. Because he had been so devoutly committed to Pharisaic tradition (Gal. 1:14) and because he refers to someone who could have been his wife's mother (Rom. 16:13), we may assume that he was once married. His statement here to the previously married confirms that—"even as I." Perhaps he was a widower. He does not identify with the virgins in verse 25 but with the unmarried and widows, that is, with the formerly married. God gave Paul the gift of celibacy and with it the ability to be single and not be preoccupied with sex and marriage.

C. The Ideal Proposal

Paul continues his proposal for singleness in verse 25, "Now concerning virgins, I have no commandment of the Lord; yet I give my judgment, as one that hath obtained mercy of the Lord to be faithful." Paul is communicating that the Lord Jesus never said anything specifically about virgins and never told anyone to get married. He simply spoke about the institution of marriage as it already existed. Yet Paul is going to add revelation as one who had obtained mercy from the Lord. He says in verses 26-27, "I suppose therefore, that this is good for the present distress, I say, that it is good for a man so to be. Art thou bound unto a wife? Seek not to be loosed. Art thou loosed from a wife? Seek not a wife."

Paul was informing the Corinthian believers that from a practical standpoint, it would be to their advantage to remain as they were. Considering the sexually debauched society in which they lived, the Corinthians were better off to remain in the state in which they came to Christ. If you are married, stay that way, and if you are not, don't seek to be. Paul adds a comfort to those who desire marriage in verse 28: "If thou marry, thou hast not sinned." Paul is saying that it is no sin if a virgin marries, but it might be to his or her advantage to stay single. He says further in verse 28, "Nevertheless, such shall have trouble in the flesh; but I spare you." Paul is writing to spare them the trouble that marriage brings. Don't marry if it isn't a necessity for you. You won't sin if you do marry, but if God has given you the ability to be single, cherish that ability because of its lack of encumbrance. This is a special gift that renders you capable of serving God in a unique way.

1. The pressure involved

There are many pressures in being single in today's society, especially with all the current emphasis on marriage and the family. It has been said that loneliness for single people is at its height during the holiday season. Many single parents often feel that way. But you don't have to feel that way. If God has given you the gift of celibacy, accept that as His plan. Since He is a loving and all-wise God, He has your best interest at heart, whether you recognize it or not. There is nothing wrong with being single.

2. The price involved

There are many advantages in being single. It provides many opportunities for service to Christ. It is wrong to force those who are content with their singleness into questioning God about their desire to remain that way.

a) Matthew 19:10-12—Jesus was speaking to the disciples and they concluded that it would be better to remain single. Jesus had just given some poignant statements concerning marriage and divorce. His disciples replied, "If the case of the man be so with his wife, it is not good to marry" (v. 10). They concluded it would be better never to get married to begin with. Jesus responded positively but reiterated that not all men could accept this statement—only those to whom it was given (vv. 11-12). The Lord indicated it would be good to stay single but noted that everyone isn't designed for that. Being single affords much potential for service to the Lord. We should never take someone who is content in being single and force them into marriage.

b) Luke 2:36-37—"There was one Anna, a prophetess, the daughter of Phanuel, of the tribe of Asher; she was of a great age, and had lived with an husband seven years from her virginity; and she was a widow of about fourscore and four years, who departed not from the temple, but served God with fastings and prayers night and day." This is one of the most beautiful stories associated with Jesus' birth and infancy. When Mary and Joseph brought the baby

Jesus to the Temple to present Him to the Lord and to offer a sacrifice, the prophetess Anna recognized Jesus as the Messiah. Her husband had lived only seven years after their marriage, and she remained a widow. At the age of eighty-four she was still faithfully serving the Lord in the Temple.

She did not look on her lot as inferior and certainly not as meaningless. She had the gift of singleness and used it joyfully in the Lord's work. God may cause you to lose your partner by death, and He may also choose from that time on for you to never marry again. If God gives you the gift to be satisfied and at peace with yourself as a single person, even though you had once been married, accept that from God. There is nothing wrong with being single. You can have a fulfilled life of complete devotion to Christ.

3. The problems involved

Paul goes on to say in verse 9, "If they cannot have self-control, let them marry; for it is better to marry than to burn." If a Christian is single but does not have the gift of singleness and is being strongly tempted sexually, he or she should pursue marriage. Paul was saying that staying single is not wrong, neither is becoming married and staying married. But in view of the "present distress"— the pressure from the world that was being applied to them—Corinthian believers who were single were probably in a much better position to remain as they were (7:25-28).

a) Man's sinful nature

Many who feel they do not have the gift of celibacy are frustrated because they can't seem to find a marriage partner. One of the problems could be that there is sin in your life that you need to deal with. Perhaps God's Word is being violated, thereby disqualifying you from pursuing His will. It could also be that you have sinned in the past and are now reaping the consequences of that sin.

b) Man's selfish nature

Another problem people face is selfishness. Don't be preoccupied with yourself; be preoccupied with the Lord. The best way to find the right person is to be the right person. If you are not the right person, you will never meet the right partner.

If you are living a righteous life and do not have the gift of singleness, God will provide a partner for you. How could God want you to be married and yet not provide a partner?

4. The precept involved

In verse 9 Paul gives a command to those who do not have the gift of singleness: "Let them marry; for it is better to marry than to burn." The Greek phrase translated "Let them marry" is an aorist imperative command. Paul is saying, "Get married." The phrase "to burn" means "to be inflamed" and is best understood as referring to strong passion (see also Rom. 1:27). A person cannot live a happy life, much less serve the Lord, if he is continually burning with sexual desire—even if the desire never results in actual immorality.

I believe that once a Christian couple decides to get married, they should do it fairly soon. Once you've made that kind of commitment, you put yourself in a position to be tempted and possibly compromise your standards. Marriage was designed to help you be fulfilled sexually. The practical problems of an early marriage are not nearly as serious as the danger of immorality. I do not advocate simply jumping into marriage for only one reason— sexual fulfillment—but there is no advantage to long engagements. In a day of lowered standards and constant suggestiveness, it is extremely difficult to stay sexually pure. Parents who encourage their engaged children to wait for several years before marrying also run the risk of putting them in a potentially tempting situation. If their commitment is to marriage, it is best for them to marry than to burn with passion.

What to Do While You Wait for Marriage

There are several thing Christians can do to control themselves sexually before marriage.

1. Channel your energy through physical work and spiritual ministry.

Idle moments do not help. Avoid listening to, looking at, or being around anything that strengthens the temptation to sin sexually. Program your mind to focus only on that which is good and helpful (Phil. 4:8).

2. Don't seek to be married for the sake of being married.

   You run a great risk of marrying the wrong person that way. Seek to love, and let marriage be a natural response. Seek to honor Christ in your life and in all your relationships, and let God bring about a marriage.

3. Let go of the sex-mad, adulterous world.

   Be careful of what you let into your senses—what you see, what you hear, and where you go. Whatever you allow in your mind is going to have a great impact on you.

4. Program your mind with the Word of God.

   Your behavior is a direct result of what you put in your mind. Pray for purity and stay in the Word.

5. Count on divine enablement to live without sexual fulfillment.

   Until God gives you the right person, He will provide strength for you to resist temptation. Paul says in 1 Corinthians 10:13, "God is faithful, who will not allow you to be tempted beyond what you are able, but with the temptation will provide the way of escape also, that you may be able to endure it" (NASB*).

6. Avoid potentially tempting situations.

   Even though you may feel you can handle such a situation, you may not be able to control someone else.

7. Praise and thank God in the midst of your singleness.

   Be content in what God is doing in your life now, not always being concerned with what will happen in the future.

8. Be accountable to a close Christian friend of the same sex.

   Don't live alone, travel alone, or go places alone where you will be vulnerable. Stay accountable to someone who is mature and who understands your needs.

II. GUIDELINES FOR CHRISTIANS MARRIED TO OTHER CHRISTIANS (vv. 10-11)

"And unto the married I command, yet not I, but the Lord, Let

New American Standard Bible.

not the wife depart from her husband; But and if she depart, let her remain unmarried, or be reconciled to her husband; and let not the husband put away his wife."

No distinction is made regarding the type of marriage involved. And as we saw in the last chapter, there were at least four marital arrangements ranging from the common-law *usus* to the noble Roman *confarreatio*. The phrase "unto the married" covers each type of marriage in the Roman system. The issue is not the kind of marriage but staying in whatever situation you found yourself when you came to Christ. Paul must be speaking about Christian marriages in verses 10-11 because in verses 12-16 he deals specifically with marriages in which only one partner is a believer. Also, Paul never gave commands (v. 10) to nonbelievers, other than to repent.

A. The Lord's Command (v. 10)

Lest there be any question about Paul's authority, he quotes the specific commands of Christ concerning marriage and divorce. Jesus, quoting Genesis 2:24, says, "For this cause shall a man leave father and mother, and shall cleave to his wife, and the two shall be one flesh. . . . They are no more two, but one flesh. What, therefore, God hath joined together, let no man put asunder" (Matt. 19:5-6). In all three passages concerning Jesus' teaching on marriage and divorce (Matt. 5:27-32; 19:3-9; Mark 10:11-12), He explicitly commanded that marriage was to be lifelong. Jesus explained that God allowed Moses to permit divorce only because of the people's hardness of heart. Divorce was permissible only in the case of adultery (Matt. 5:31-32). God hates divorce (Mal. 2:16). Divorce is contrary to God's plan for mankind, and when allowed in cases of adultery, is only a gracious concession to the innocent party in an irreconcilable case of unfaithfulness. Where there is repentance, there can always be restoration.

It is likely that some Corinthian Christians had decided they should get a divorce for "spiritual" reasons. Paul had to instruct them on the proper view of marriage or else many would use that excuse to rid themselves of the partner they didn't want. Paul was not discussing divorce based on adultery; Jesus made a provision for that (Matt. 5:32; 19:8-9). He was talking about divorce for any other reason— even supposedly spiritual ones.

54

B. The Apostle's Command (v. 11)

Some of the believers in Corinth had already divorced one another or were moving toward that end. Paul instructs, "If she depart, let her remain unmarried, or be reconciled to her husband; and let not the husband put away his wife." Paul was explaining that if a Christian divorces another Christian, neither partner is free to remarry (except in the case of adultery). They must stay single or rejoin their former mate. In God's eyes that union has never been broken.

1. The reiteration

Except for fornication (Matt. 5:32; 19:1-9), there can be no divorce. The only grounds Jesus ever gave for the dissolution of marriage was sexual immorality. That is clear in the case of Joseph and Mary. Matthew 1:19 says, "Joseph, her husband, being a just man, and not willing to make her a public example, was minded to put her away privately." Joseph was shocked when he found out Mary was pregnant. He knew they had had no sexual relations and wanted to protect Mary from the embarrassment of being caught in adultery. Joseph had the option to divorce Mary if she had become pregnant by another man. Because Joseph was a just man, he desired to act righteously by divorcing his wife, whom he thought had committed adultery. The wonderful thing was that the Holy Spirit had conceived within her the Christ child. Mary had been vindicated.

2. The reinforcement

The case Paul describes in 1 Corinthians 7:10-11 does not discuss adultery. The command is that if a divorce occurred that was not on the basis of adultery, reconciliation or remaining single are the only options. If you have divorced already, then you must stay single or be reconciled to your husband. The union God had established was never broken. Corinthian believers who were endeavoring to be obedient to Christ were sure to attempt to be reconciled to their spouses.

III. GUIDELINES FOR CHRISTIANS MARRIED TO UNBELIEVERS WHO WANT TO STAY (vv. 12-14)

"But to the rest speak I, not the Lord, If any brother hath a wife that believeth not, and she be pleased to dwell with him, let him not put her away. And the woman who hath an husband that believeth not, and if he be pleased to dwell with her, let her not leave him. For the unbelieving husband is sanctified by the wife, and the unbelieving wife is sanctified by the husband; else were your children unclean, but now are they holy."

A. The Questions

Another natural question that arose in the Corinthian church was whether new Christians were to remain married to non-Christians, especially those who were immoral and idolatrous pagans. Were they free to divorce the one to whom they were unequally yoked? In light of Paul's teaching in 1 Corinthians 6:15-20, their bodies were now members of Christ and were temples of the Holy Spirit. The Corinthians were justifiably concerned about whether to maintain their marriage or divorce their mate to please the Lord. Some might have thought that to continue in their unequally-yoked relationship meant to join Christ to Satan, defiling the believer and his children and dishonoring the Lord. The desire for a Christian partner would be strong.

B. The Answers

The first thing that needs to be understood is that mixed marriages can be prevented if, as a Christian, you marry "only in the Lord" (v. 39). Mixed marriages are forbidden when they can be prevented. The idea of a Christian marrying a non-Christian is antithetical to Scripture (2 Cor. 6:14). The question Paul addressed is what happens when one of the spouses in a marriage relationship comes to Christ. What are they to do?

1. The authority

Jesus had not taught directly about that problem, and so Paul said, "To the rest speak I, not the Lord" (v. 12). That is not a denial of inspiration or an indication that Paul is giving only his own opinion. It is merely to say that God had not given any previous revelation on the subject, but Paul was now setting it forth.

2. The affirmation

Paul went on to say, "If any brother hath a wife that believeth not, and she be pleased to dwell with him, let him not put her away. And the woman who hath an husband that believeth not, and if he be pleased to dwell with her, let her not leave him" (vv. 12-13). God doesn't want people to be saved and then use that as an excuse to divorce their spouse. The Corinthians were not to divorce their mate, even to marry a Christian.

The early church was being accused of destroying family relationships by encouraging believers to divorce their spouses. Many unsaved husbands were upset when their wives were saved because for a woman to change her religion apart from her husband was unthinkable. Most often each member of the household shared a common faith. Tertullian wrote about heathen husbands being angry with their Christian wives because they wanted to kiss martyrs' bonds, embrace Christian brothers and sisters, and go along the streets to the cottages of the poor to meet their needs. One can sympathize with an unsaved husband whose wife was not behaving as she should. The apostle Paul's command is if you have a partner who doesn't believe in Christ but wants to stay with you, don't divorce him or her.

3. The agency

Paul says, "The unbelieving husband is sanctified by the wife, and the unbelieving wife is sanctified by the husband; else were your children unclean, but now are they holy" (v. 14). Christians married to unbelievers were not to worry that they themselves, their marriage, or their children would be defiled by the unbelieving spouse. In fact, the opposite is the case. Both the children and the unbelieving spouse would be sanctified through the believing wife or husband.

In this context, the word *sanctified* does not refer to salvation; otherwise the spouse would not be spoken of as unbelieving. It refers to being set apart. The words translated "sanctified" and "holy" are from the same Greek root. The sanctification that Paul talks about here is matrimonial and familial, not personal or spiritual. You become personally and spiritually sanctified only when you believe in Christ. But having a Christian living in your home has a sanctifying influence on the other members of the family. One Christian in the home graces the entire home. Such a home is not Christian in the full sense, but it is immeasurably superior to one that is totally unbelieving. The indwelling Spirit and all the blessings and graces that flow into the believer's life from heaven will spill over to enrich all who are near.

Although the believer's faith cannot suffice for the salvation of anyone but himself, he is often the means whereby other family members come to Christ by the power of his testimony. For instance, two people in marriage become one flesh. Even if God blesses the one Christian, the unsaved will receive some of God's blessing as a result. Marriage to a Christian creates a relationship to God for the non-Christian, and even though it is short of salvation, it is far superior to pagan life.

A young woman came up to me after the service one Sunday morning and told me that when she was growing up, her grandmother was the only Christian in the family. The grandmother always spoke of her love for Christ and witnessed to the family in what she said and by what she did. Eventually, three of the four grandchildren came to know the Lord, and each one declared that their grandmother had the greatest influence on their decision for Christ.

a) Genesis 18:26—"The Lord said, If I find in Sodom fifty righteous within the city, then I will spare all the place for their sakes." When Abraham could not find that many, he pleaded with God to reduce the number to forty-five, then forty, and finally all the way down to ten. In each case the Lord agreed to spare the city, but not even ten righteous could be found. The point is that God was willing to bless many wicked people for the sake even of a few of His own people in their midst.

b) 1 Kings 15:4—This verse says, "Nevertheless, for David's sake, did the Lord his God give him a lamp in Jerusalem, to set up his son after him, and to establish Jerusalem." God declared that because of David, He was going to bless Jerusalem. That city hadn't done anything to deserve God's blessing, but because of David's faithfulness He would bless Israel.

Likewise, in a home where there is only one Christian, others in the home benefit from the blessings of God. If you are not a Christian but your partner is, you need to thank God that you live in a home where God is at work. It is similar to your spouse receiving a huge inheritance—you have nothing to do with it. You aren't even related to the giver; nevertheless, you receive the gift also. Paul is saying it is a blessed thing for an unbeliever to be married to a Christian. If you are a Christian and your partner wants to stay, let him stay and sense the blessing of God on your own life. Sanctifying matrimonial grace might lead to saving grace.

4. The advantage

Paul goes a step further in proving his point by arguing in reverse. He says, "Else were your children unclean, but now are they holy." The Christian need not fear that his children will be defiled by the unbelieving father or mother. God promises that the opposite is true. They would certainly be unclean if both parents were unbelievers. The Lord guarantees that the presence of just one Christian parent will help influence the children spiritually. It is not that their salvation is assured but that they are protected from undue spiritual harm and are bound to receive some sort of spiritual blessing. Evidently, some of the Corinthians were worried that since their mate was not saved, they were defiling their children. If you and your children are subjected to a non-Christian influence in the home, pray that God will use you as a godly influence to bring them to full faith in Jesus Christ.

IV. GUIDELINES FOR CHRISTIANS MARRIED TO UNBELIEVERS WHO WANT TO LEAVE (vv. 15-16)

"But if the unbelieving depart, let him depart. A brother or a sister is not under bondage in such cases; but God hath called us to peace. For what knowest thou, O wife, whether thou shalt save thy husband? Or how knowest thou, O man, whether thou shalt save thy wife?

A. God's Call to Part (v. 15a)

If an unbelieving spouse wants to divorce his mate, Paul's command is to "let him depart." The Greek construction of the verb is in the middle voice which means, "If the unbeliever takes himself out of the marriage relationship, let him depart." This is a case where the unbeliever initiates the divorce proceedings. If that occurs, the Christian partner is not to contest it. The Greek word for "depart" is chōrizō. It refers to divorce. The believer is not to fight the divorce.

B. God's Call to Peace (v. 15b)

Paul explains why the believing partner should not contest divorce proceedings: "A brother or a sister is not under bondage in such cases; but God hath called us to peace." In

God's sight, the bond between a husband and wife is dissolved only by death (Rom. 7:2), adultery (Matt. 5:32; 19:1-9), or an unbeliever's departure. Paul is saying that a divorce initiated by the nonbelieving spouse is permitted, especially when it occurs because of the believing spouse's testimony for Christ. You are free from the bondage of continuing in a marriage relationship with a spouse who is determined to leave. When a divorce occurs for that reason, or for the other reasons stated above, you are free to remarry. Throughout Scripture, whenever legitimate divorce occurs, remarriage is assumed. When divorce is permitted, remarriage is permitted. (However, it is clearly forbidden in the case presented by verse 11).

The reason for going through with a divorce initiated by an unbeliever is that "God hath called us to peace." One of the benefits of being a Christian is living a peaceful life with God. There is nothing that God needs less than constant fighting, tension, and frustration in the home. A home in turmoil is not God's objective for the Christian, nor is marriage primarily a foundation for evangelism. You cannot say whether you are going to lead your spouse to Christ or not (v. 16). You may even drive him farther from Christ. If he wants to leave, let him. It would be better to reject Christianity because of Christ, not because of your poor testimony.

C. God's Call to Patience (v. 16)

Paul deals with the obvious objection of the conscientious Christian in verse 16: "What knowest thou, O wife, whether thou shalt save thy husband? Or how knowest thou, O man, whether thou shalt save thy wife?" Someone will invariably say, "If I don't keep my marriage together, who's going to reach my unsaved spouse?" Many Christians have tried to keep a marriage together even when the spouse was unbelieving and wanted a divorce, but that of course is against God's will. A wife has no assurance that she will save her husband, and a husband has no assurance that he will save his wife. Regardless of a Christian's motives and hopes, the likelihood of leading an antagonistic partner to Christ is minimal. If the partner stays in the marriage unwillingly or reluctantly, the disruption of family peace is assured. Verse 15 is a command, not an option.

It is God alone who saves people. And one thing that God has never needed is quarrelsome, angry, hostile homes in which to save people. Marriage is not primarily an instrument for evangelism, especially if the unbelieving partner wants to leave. The believer should let God pursue the spouse's soul with the message of salvation, and use whomever He wills to bring his spouse to faith in Him.

Conclusion

Throughout 1 Corinthians 7, the apostle Paul has given many guidelines concerning singleness and marriage. Some of the questions posed at the beginning of the lesson can now be answered:

1. Is marriage a command?

   Marriage is not a command in Scripture. It is good to be married, but it is not commanded for everyone.

2. Do you have to be married to please God?

   No. Pleasing God is as a result of obedience to Him, regardless of your marital status.

3. Should single people marry or is it more spiritual to stay single?

   Paul affirms that it is good to remain single. It is a gift given by God to be used for His glory (but not one that everyone possesses).

4. Are you a more devoted Christian if you are not married?

   No. If you have the gift of singleness, devote your life to Christ. But if you have difficulty controlling your sexual desires, then God probably intends for you to be married. If so, get married and devote your life to Christ.

5. Should married people who have subsequently come to Christ abstain from sex?

   Paul clearly commands that those who are married are obligated to fulfill the sexual aspect of their marriage. You are not to deprive each other of the need for sexual fulfillment.

6. Should a Christian married to a non-Christian get a divorce?

   If you are married to an unbeliever who wants to stay, let him stay and let him and your children be graced with the blessing that comes from God through you. If you are married to an unbeliever who wants to leave, let him leave, because God has called you to live a life of peace.

Don't worry about saving the soul of your mate; that is God's job. It is likely that nagging your unbelieving spouse to stay would further compound the problem, not help it. God knows about the situation and will work out His own way.

Focusing on the Facts

1. What is Paul's purpose in writing the seventh chapter of 1 Corinthians (see p. 46)?
2. What did the Jewish leaders believe about marriage (see p. 47)?
3. Is marriage a command from Scripture? Explain your answer (see p. 47).
4. True or false: Those who have a strong desire for sexual fulfillment most likely do not have the gift of singleness (see p. 47).
5. What four groups of people does Paul address in verses 8-16 (see p. 48)?
6. Who are "the unmarried"? What is Paul's response to them and the widows in verses 8-9 (see pp. 48-49)?
7. Single people are _____ in Christianity to help _____ the plan of God (see p. 48).
8. Explain why the apostle Paul had probably been married in the past (see p. 49).
9. What are the advantages of remaining single (see p. 50)?
10. What are the potential problems of remaining single (see pp. 51-52)?
11. Several things were mentioned that could prevent someone from knowing whether or not they have the gift of singleness. What were they (see p. 51)?
12. What are several things Christians can do while they wait for marriage (see pp. 52-53)?
13. What kind of marriage situation does Paul address in verses 10-11 (see p. 54)?
14. What was Jesus' teaching concerning marriage and divorce (see p. 54)?
15. If a Christian divorces another Christian, not on the grounds of adultery, does he or she have the right to remarry someone else (see p. 55)?
16. Are believers supposed to remain married to nonbelievers, especially those living with immoral and even idolatrous partners (see p. 56)?
17. Can a person who is already a Christian before marriage marry a non-Christian? Support your answer with Scripture (see p. 56).
18. What is meant by the unbelieving spouse or children being sanctified by the believing partner (see pp. 57-58)?

19. What is Paul's command to a believing spouse whose unbelieving partner wants to leave (see p. 59)?
20. List the three grounds the New Testament gives for remarriage (see pp. 59-60).
21. What reason does Paul give for not hindering an unsaved spouse who wants a divorce (see p. 60)?
22. How would you respond to the person who says, "If I don't keep my marriage together, who's going to reach my unsaved spouse?" (see p. 60)?
23. Answer in your own words the following questions: Is marriage a command? Do you have to be married to please God? Should single people marry, or is it more spiritual to remain single (see p. 61)?
24. What is God's view concerning sexual fulfillment with those who are married? Should a Christian married to a non-Christian get a divorce (see p. 61)?

Pondering the Principles

1. The first set of guidelines we discussed was for single Christians in 1 Corinthians 7:8-9. Paul's recommendation to the formerly married and widows was that they remain single, as he did. Paul also recognized that if they desired marriage, they needed to marry, for it is better to marry than to burn with sexual passion. Are you a widow or have you been married in the past before coming to Christ? If either one is the case, ask God to make it clear to you what He wants to do in this regard. Consider Paul's recommendation to remain single. In whatever situation you eventually find yourself, devote the remainder of your life to serving Christ.

2. The second set of guidelines was for Christians married to other Christians (vv. 10-11). The apostle Paul quotes the Lord Himself and states that at no time are Christians ever to divorce for any supposed spiritual reasons. Jesus stated that marriage is to be lifelong. Spirituality has nothing to do with your marital status. Paul also commanded that if divorce had occurred without biblical grounds, either remaining single or reconciliation were the only options. Have you divorced your Christian spouse on non-biblical grounds? If so, you are either to remain single or be reconciled to that person. If you've already violated the Lord's commands as a Christian by being illegitimately divorced and remarried, you have only one recourse—confess your sin, telling God and those you have wronged the sorrow of your heart, and

remain in the union you are now in. See if God will not make something sweet out of the bitter.

3. The third set of guidelines covered in verses 12-14 is for Christians married to unbelievers who wanted to stay married. If you have been married before coming to Christ and your unbelieving spouse desires to stay with you, do not seek a divorce. You have a unique opportunity to be salt and light to that person. According to verse 14, you have the responsibility to be a sanctifying influence in your home, both to your spouse and children. Memorize 1 Peter 3:1-2, 7 and ask God to use you to help bring your loved ones to Christ.

4. The fourth set of guidelines is in verses 15-16, and is for Christians married to unbelievers who want to divorce. Paul's command is clear: If you are a believer, and your unbelieving spouse is determined to divorce you, do not stop him. You are not to fight the divorce, for that may lead to further harm rather than good. If your unbelieving partner leaves, search the heart of God concerning your future status. Pray that God in His sovereignty will bring your spouse to faith in Christ and bring about the reconciliation of your marriage. If you feel that you cannot remain unmarried, ask God to bring you a mate who loves Christ and is committed to Him.

4
Christians and Social Revolution

Outline

Introduction
A. The Basis
B. The Background
   1. The Jewish philosophy
   2. The Gentile philosophy

Lesson
I. Christianity Is Not Social Revolution (vv. 17-19)
  A. The Principle of Remaining as You Are (v. 17)
    1. The intention
    2. The impact
    3. The insurrection
    4. The influence
    5. The implication
    6. The indication
  B. The Practice of Becoming Circumcised or Uncircumcised (vv. 18-19)
    1. The recognition
    2. The reason
    3. The reverse
    4. The result
II. Christianity Is Not Social Resistance (vv. 20-23)
  A. The Principles (v. 20)
    1. Be content
    2. Be realistic
  B. The Practice (v. 21a)
    1. Ephesians 6:5-8
    2. Colossians 3:22-24
  C. The Parallel (v. 21)
    1. The slaves of Rome
    2. The slave of Philemon
  D. The Paradox (v. 22)

Introduction

A. The Basis

Much has been said and written about the social role and responsibility of the church. At times throughout church history, and especially in our own day, people have claimed that Christianity should be an agent of external social reform, even of revolution if necessary. Many sincere Christians have wondered what their role should be in social activism, and whether it is biblically justified. What are Christians, individually or collectively, to do about wrongs and abuses in civil systems and social practices? Paul addresses those issues in 1 Corinthians 7:17-24.

B. The Background

Marriage is the overall context of 1 Corinthians 7. Although the Bible has much to say about marriage, it also talks about those who are single, divorced, and widowed. It has much to say about what is required within a marriage, including God's standards for the husband, wife, and the children. A portion of what is in the Word of God concerning marriage is here in the seventh chapter of 1 Corinthians.

1. The Jewish philosophy

The Corinthian Christians were having many problems in the area of marriage. The problems arose from pressure that was being put upon them to conform to a certain view of marriage. The Jewish population believed that to remain single was to defy the law of God. They used Scripture such as Genesis 1:28 to support their point. If you were single and a new convert in Corinth, there would be tremendous pressure on you to be married. Added to that pressure was the reality that God Himself had given some of the Corinthians the gracious gift of remaining single (v. 7). Although God intended for some to remain single, the Jewish leaders were proclaiming that the only way to receive God's blessing was through marriage.

2. The Gentile philosophy

    Another pressure on the Corinthians was the Gentile
    philosophy of asceticism, the belief that singleness was
    the only way you could be totally devoted to God. It was
    thought that if you were married, you should divorce
    your spouse to be in God's will. And if you were married
    to an unbeliever, it was thought you must divorce be-
    cause you were being defiled and your children would be
    raised as half pagan and half spiritual.

Lesson

First Corinthians 7:17-24 plainly teaches the following basic
principle, which is readily applicable to the civil and social
conditions in which believers live: Christians should willingly
accept the situation into which God has placed them and be
content to serve Him there. However, human nature rebels
against that principle, so Paul states it three times in these eight
verses so that his readers could not miss the point. We should not
be preoccupied with changing our outward circumstances.

I. CHRISTIANITY IS NOT SOCIAL REVOLUTION (vv. 17-19)

    "[Only] as [the Lord] hath distributed to every man, as [God]
    hath called every one, so let him walk. And so ordain I in all the
    churches. Is any man called being circumcised? Let him not
    become uncircumcised. Is any called in uncircumcision? Let him
    not be circumcised. Circumcision is nothing, and uncircumcision
    is nothing, but the keeping of the commandments of God." (The
    brackets indicate the way the verse correctly appears in the Greek
    text.)

    A. The Principle of Remaining as You Are (v. 17)

        The apostle Paul states in this passage that the Christian life
        is not social revolution but spiritual regeneration. When you
        come to Jesus Christ, there is no reason to say, "Now that I'm
        a Christian, I have to stop being single" or, "I must dissolve
        my marriage and be celibate." Paul is not saying that you
        have to divorce your unsaved spouse because you are defiling
        yourself.

        1. The intention

            Christianity was never designed to disrupt social relation-
            ships. There were many in the Corinthian church who
            were using their Christianity as a justification for every
            kind of social change. Husbands were divorcing their

wives and vice versa, single people were being pressured into marriage when they had the gift of celibacy, and slaves were chafing under the rule of their master. Perhaps they were claiming that since Galatians 3:28 teaches there is neither male nor female, bond or free, but that all are one in Christ, they were justified in developing a revolutionary attitude. But such an attitude would have destroyed the testimony of the Corinthian assembly. For anyone to see Christianity as a social revolution would cast doubt on the reality of Christianity, which is a transformed life. When Christianity becomes closely identified with a social movement, the message of the gospel is in danger of being lost.

2. The impact

There is no question that Christianity has had a profound impact upon society. Christians have rightly been accused of being preoccupied with spiritual things, such as miracles, signs, and wonders; the spiritual equality of the sexes as well as of slave and free; and the second coming of Jesus Christ. The reality of coming judgment, eternal bliss in heaven, and disdain for earthly wealth were concepts that were hard for the world to understand. Nevertheless, Christianity has had a profound effect on society, apart from those eternal realities.

3. The insurrection

Christianity could have had a negative effect if it focused on social issues rather than spiritual issues. It was enough that the world was confused about theology without confusing them further by making Christianity merely a social enterprise. Paul wanted to make sure that the church kept its proper perspective. There is a need to be involved in certain social issues but not at the expense of losing the gospel in the process. Christianity in and of itself is not a justification to overthrow the government. When that occurs, you become like every other revolution to overthrow the government and the distinctiveness of the gospel is lost.

4. The influence

Being involved in spiritual concerns doesn't disqualify Christians from involvement in social causes. Christians individually and corporately are to minister in many ways, including the practical, ·material ways of feeding the hungry and helping heal the sick and injured. Christianity has been a leader in building hospitals and orphanages, in visiting prisoners, in helping the poor, and in ministering in countless other ways that are considered social services. But those are ministries of individual Christians, not services that they persuade society to perform.

Paul endeavors to show in this passage that being a Christian does not destroy homes or ruin friendships. It does not mean creating chaos by destroying the institutions in which you live. A relationship to Christ is compatible with any social status. Within Christianity, you can be single, married, widowed, divorced, slave, free, Jewish, or Gentile. You can live in any kind of society, whether a democracy or total dictatorship. Whether you live in America, Cuba, China, or the Soviet Union, Christianity is still compatible with your social status. The reason is that Christianity is internal, not external.

Paul was trying to show the Corinthians not to use Christianity as a justification to misrepresent the truth. If a wife becomes a Christian, she should be a better wife, not a rebellious one. And if a husband becomes a Christian, he should be a better husband. Likewise, if there is a slave who becomes a Christian, he should be a better slave, not a social revolutionary. You can be a Christian in any society because Christianity is a spiritual relationship to the living God, and it has little or nothing to do with your social status.

5. The implication

The principle that Paul lays down was not meant to be a universal command with no exceptions. He is not saying that if you were thirteen years old when you came to Christ and single, you have to stay single the rest of your life. It was meant as a general principle, not an absolute law. Paul himself says in verse 10 that if you are married, stay that way. But then he gives an exception in verse 15: "If the unbelieving depart, let him depart." Likewise, Paul gives the general rule in verse 17: "As the Lord hath distributed to every man, as God hath called every one, so let him walk." If you are a slave, stay that way, but if you have the opportunity to gain your freedom, take it. Paul is teaching you not to be preoccupied with the problem of your social status, even if you are a slave, and as a result, create social turmoil.

The overarching reason is again in verse 15: "God hath called us to peace." In whatever state we find ourselves, we are to create peace, not social revolution. It should be obvious that Paul is not telling believers to stay in occupations, professions, or habits that are inherently immoral or illegal. A thief is not to keep stealing, a prostitute is not to continue in prostitution, nor is a drunkard to continue to drink. Everything sinful is to be forsaken. The issue for believers is to be content in the social situations in which they found themselves when they were saved.

Should Christians Overthrow Ungodly Governments?

Many have said, "The Christians in the Soviet Union should overthrow the government." My response is always, "Why? What biblical justification is there for a Christian revolution like the Bolshevik revolution that brought about the communist state?" Russian believers can be salt and light within their communist society. When God is ready to change that society, the roots of Christianity spreading through it may bring about its downfall. But when Christianity turns into a social issue, you have what's happening in Northern Ireland—and the testimony of Christianity is destroyed. It is better that the church leaven society with biblical truth rather than guns, which only confuse the issue. God has called Christians to peace (1 Cor. 7:15). Stay in whatever situation you find yourself. Jesus said, "Blessed are the peacemakers" (Matt. 5:9).

a) Romans 12:18—Paul said, "If it be possible, as much as lieth in you, live peaceably with all men."

b) Romans 14:19—Paul also said, "Let us, therefore, follow after the things which make for peace."

c) 2 Corinthians 13:11—Paul said, "Live in peace; and the God of love and peace shall be with you."

d) Hebrews 12:14—The author of Hebrews says, "Follow peace with all men."

e) James 3:17—James said, "The wisdom that is from above is first pure, then peaceable, gentle, and easy to be entreated, full of mercy and good fruits, without partiality, and without hypocrisy." If you are exemplifying and communicating divine wisdom, you will

70

bring about righteousness and pervade the world with peace.

f) 2 Timothy 2:22-25—Paul told Timothy to "follow righteousness, faith, love, peace" (v. 22). He went on to say how: "In meekness instructing those that oppose [you], if God, perhaps, will give them repentance to the acknowledging of the truth." If you are peaceful, patient, and gentle, God will use your testimony to bring people to Christ. The way to evangelize the world is not through social revolution but spiritual regeneration.

Christ made it clear that He did not come to instigate an external social revolution, as the Jewish people of His day thought the Messiah would. Jesus told Pilate, "My kingdom is not of this world. If My kingdom were of this world, then My servants would be fighting, that I might not be delivered up to the Jews; but as it is, My kingdom is not of this realm" (John 18:36, NASB). Christ's mission was "to seek and to save that which was lost" (Luke 19:10), and that is the mission of His church.

6. The indication

Paul starts verse 17 by saying, "[Only] as [the Lord] hath distributed to every man." The Greek verb for "distributed" is *memeriken*, which means "to bestow" or "to apportion to one his share of something." Paul is saying that if you are a slave, it is the Lord who has apportioned to you that position. Whatever the Lord has allotted to you—be it singleness, marriage, or slavery—continue to walk in that calling. God does not expect a Christian to suddenly discontinue his job or marital status. He has you there for a reason. "Let's show the world," Paul says in effect, "that Christianity brings solidarity to society, not chaos."

B. The Practice of Becoming Circumcised or Uncircumcised (vv. 18-19)

After stating the principle in verse 17, Paul illustrates it in verses 18-19: "Is any man called being circumcised? Let him not become uncircumcised. Is any called in uncircumcision? Let him not be circumcised. Circumcision is nothing, and uncircumcision is nothing, but the keeping of the commandments of God." In the epistles, the term *called* refers to an

71

effectual call to salvation. Paul is saying that when a Jewish person is saved, he should not try to become like a Gentile.

1. The recognition

Circumcision was an embarrassment in the Roman world. According to the apocryphal Maccabean works, which were written during the intertestamental period, some Jewish men made themselves uncircumcised (1 Macc. 1:11-16). Josephus tells us that during the Greek rule of the eastern Mediterranean several centuries before Christ, some Jewish men who wanted to be accepted into Greek society had surgery performed to make themselves appear uncircumcised when they bathed or exercised at the gymnasiums. The Roman encyclopedist Celsius, in the first century A.D., wrote a detailed description of the surgical procedure for uncircumcision (*De Medicina* VII. 25).

The practice was so common that considerable rabbinic literature addressed the problem (e.g., *Aboth* 3:11; *Jerushalmi Peah* 1 and 16; *Lamentations Rabbah* 1:20). Jewish men who had such surgery were referred to as *epispatics*, a name taken from the euphemistic term *epispaomai*, meaning "to draw over," or "to pull towards." That is the term Paul uses here for the word *uncircumcised*.

2. The reason

Perhaps some Jewish Christians thought this unusual surgery was a way to demonstrate their break with Judaism. They wanted to identify with the Greeks' social status. But Paul is saying if you are Jewish and come to Christ, you are to remain Jewish. Paul's reasoning is clear: the most likely person for a Jew to lead to Christ is another Jewish person, especially someone in his own household. But if he comes to Christ and immediately renounces his Judaism, he will damage his testimony to his people. If he desires to become uncircumcised and removes the mark of the covenant of God with His people, he would alienate himself from the harvest field that he is most capable of reaching.

For Jews to want to appear as Gentiles or for Gentiles to subscribe to things unique to Jews is wrong both in a spiritual and practical sense. It is wrong spiritually because it adds an outward form to the gospel that has no spiritual merit or meaning and is something the Lord

does not require. It is wrong practically because it unnec-
essarily separates believers from their families and
friends and makes witnessing to them much more difficult.

3. The reverse

In verse 18 Paul reverses the principle to apply to the new
Gentile converts: "Is any called in uncircumcision? Let
him not be circumcised." Gentiles who become Christians are not to become like Jews. The problem concerning circumcision was not as serious in Corinth as it was in
Galatia, where Judaizers taught that circumcision was
necessary for salvation (Gal. 5:2-3). In Corinth the practice may have been viewed as a mark of special recognition or blessing from God. But Paul is saying that
circumcision is not necessary either for salvation or
blessing. It has no spiritual significance or value for
Christians at all.

4. The result

Paul says in verse 19, "Circumcision is nothing, and
uncircumcision is nothing, but the keeping of the commandments of God." The only issue Paul sees here is
spiritual, not social. Obedience is the only mark of
faithfulness that the Lord recognizes. It is sometimes
costly, but it is always possible, no matter what your
circumstances may be. The issue is internal, not external.

II. CHRISTIANITY IS NOT SOCIAL RESISTANCE (vv. 20-23)

"Let every man abide in the same calling in which he was called.
Art thou called, being a servant? Care not for it; but if thou
mayest be made free, use it rather. For he that is called in the
Lord, being a servant, is the Lord's freeman; likewise also he that
is called, being free, is Christ's servant. Ye are bought with a
price; be not ye the servants of men."

A. The Principles (v. 20)

1. Be content

For the second time Paul states the principle of being
content to stay in the condition you were in when you
were saved, whether racial or social. Paul is again com-
manding that Christians need to be preoccupied with
spiritual things, not their social standing, even if it means
remaining a slave.

Those of us living in America with its many freedoms tend to think of ourselves as mature in comparison to other believers around the world. But there are no doubt Christians in communistic countries who are more mature spiritually. They are often more devoted to Jesus Christ and realize even more of the blessing of God because of their persecution.

2. Be realistic

It needs to be stated, however, that the apostle Paul is not saying a person, upon receiving Christ, can never seek to progress. A Christian can seek a promotion, advance in his education, or even seek to increase his income, all of course, with a proper motive. The apostle here is merely emphasizing that you're not to try to change your social status just because you have embraced Christ and expect to have justice immediately prevail on earth. Christianity is compatible with any kind of social structure, as long as the Christian realizes the key ingredient is to keep the commands of Christ, one of which is to obey the government (Rom. 13:1-7). You may have to pay a higher price for your faith in a harsher country, but Christianity is possible anywhere. When the Lord saved you, He didn't save you primarily to change your earthly status, but your eternal destiny.

B. The Practice (v. 21a)

Paul gives a second illustration, this time concerning slaves: "Art thou called, being a servant? Care not for it." Paul's point is not to approve of slavery or to suggest that it is as good a condition to live under as freedom. His point is that, if a person is a slave, he is still able to live the Christian life. He is every bit as able to obey and serve Christ in a state of slavery as in freedom. Slavery is not an obstacle to Christian living.

1. Ephesians 6:5-8—Paul gave this command: "Servants, be obedient to them that are your masters according to the flesh, with fear and trembling, in singleness of your heart, as unto Christ; not with eyeservice, as men-pleasers, but as the servants of Christ, doing the will of God from the heart, with good will doing service as to the Lord, and not to men, knowing that whatever good thing any man doeth, the same shall he receive of the Lord, whether he be bond or free." Paul said for the slave to serve his master as though he were Jesus Christ.

74

2. Colossians 3:22-24—Paul again said, "Servants, obey in all things your masters according to the flesh; not with eyeservice, as men-pleasers, but in singleness of heart, fearing God. And whatever ye do, do it heartily, as to the Lord, and not unto men, knowing that of the Lord ye shall receive the reward of the inheritance; for ye serve the Lord Christ." The Bible does not approve of slavery, but it also does not approve of Christians creating social revolution.

Slaves had a unique opportunity to testify for the Lord. They were to show their human masters that they worked hard and honestly, not because they were forced to, but because they wanted to—out of love for and obedience to their true Lord and Master. They could demonstrate true contentment and peace in the midst of slavery, thus showing the inner provision of salvation.

The important thing is to serve God regardless of your circumstances and God, through the righteous lives of many, will bring about His ends in the world. Paul's point is, if you are a slave, be a good slave, and if you're a master, be a good master. If Jesus' goal were to abolish slavery, He would have destroyed it during His earthly ministry. The focus of Christ's ministry was internal change, not external. Slavery is fine if God has called you to that status. And as Christianity penetrates into a society, the dissolution of evil social structures will result.

C. The Parallel (v. 21)

Paul says at the end of verse 21, "If thou mayest be made free, use it rather." Having affirmed the principle of contentment, Paul makes it clear that he did not consider slavery to be the most desirable state. Some people have reversed this passage to teach that even if you are offered liberty, you are more spiritual if you turn it down. But the reality is that freedom is immeasurably better than slavery. And, as a Christian, you are not more spiritual for staying in slavery. If a slave has the opportunity to become free, as did many in New Testament times, he should take advantage of it. The apostle Paul himself was content to serve the Lord in jail. He carried on much of his ministry from a jail cell. But when he was freed, he left.

1. The slaves of Rome

I read an interesting historical analysis of the slave system in Rome. I learned that the ratio of slaves to free men was probably three to one from the second century B.C. to the third century A.D. Many of them were in the process of being emancipated, and some were well educated. There were some cruel masters, but often the situation was tolerable.

2. The slave of Philemon

The book of Philemon is an excellent illustration of the point Paul was trying to make in this passage. It centers around the runaway slave Onesimus, whom Paul had led to Christ (v. 10). As it happened, Onesimus's owner, Philemon, was a Christian. He was Paul's "dearly beloved, brother and fellow worker," and the church in Colosse met in his house (vv. 1-2). Paul made a strong personal and spiritual appeal for Philemon to forgive Onesimus and to accept him back, not just as a slave, but as a Christian brother (v. 16). Yet, embarrassing as it has been to some Christian activists, Paul did not condemn slavery or question Philemon's legal rights over his slave. He did not ask for social equality for Onesimus. In fact, he even used slavery as an analogy for the believer's walk with God.

Some have criticized Paul for not attacking the system of slavery, but if Christianity had encouraged the ending of slavery, it would have been seen as a political revolution, and Christians would have been needlessly killed in a revolution. And if Christian slaves had started to disrupt society, the major issue—the gospel—would have been lost.

That is also true today. Each time Christendom has attached itself to a social movement, the message of Christianity has been lost. When the Christian life is lived out, emancipation is bound to happen. But again, Paul emphasizes that as a believer, you should not concern yourself with your earthly state. Your internal spirituality is of far more importance.

D. The Paradox (v. 22)

Paul draws an interesting paradox in verse 22: "He that is called in the Lord, being a servant, is the Lord's freeman." Paul is saying that no bondage is as terrible or enslaving as that from which Christ redeemed us. In Him we are freed from sin, Satan, judgment, hell, and the curse of the law. Every true Christian has already been delivered from the slavery of sin. In Christ we have the most complete and glorious freedom possible.

But lest those who were free when coming to Christ feel boastful or proud, Paul says, "Likewise also he that is called, being free, is Christ's servant." Our freedom in Christ is not freedom to do our own will but freedom to do His will (Rom. 6:22).

Paul is saying that those who are free when coming to Christ are to become slaves to Him. As a Christian you're the servant of Jesus Christ, yet you are no longer in bondage to sin and judgment. When we focus on our spiritual freedom and our slavery to God, we realize that our status among men is not all-important. It does not matter whether we are physically bound or free, only that we are both spiritually bound and spiritually free—the wonderful paradox of the gospel of our Lord Jesus Christ.

E. The Price (v. 23)

Paul takes the idea of slavery a step further in verse 23: "Ye are bought with a price; be not ye the servants of men." According to this verse, you do not ever have to consider yourself a slave again. You may be a slave physically, but you are no longer a slave to the ways of the world. Paul is referring to becoming slaves of the ways of men, the world, and the flesh. That is the slavery into which many of the Corinthian believers had fallen. It was this kind of slavery that caused their divisions, strife, immaturity, and immorality.

What is the price Paul is speaking about here? First Peter 1:18-19 explains: "Ye know that ye were not redeemed with corruptible things, like silver and gold, from your vain manner of life received by tradition from your fathers, but with the precious blood of Christ, as of a lamb without blemish and without spot." We have been bought by God, and we belong to Him. We must never become the moral and spiritual slaves of men, living by their standards and seeking to please them.

III. CHRISTIANITY IS NOT SOCIAL REBELLION (v. 24)

"Brethren, let every man, in whatever state he is called, there abide with God."

A. The Principle Reiterated

For the third time in this passage, the apostle Paul gives the following principle: Christians should willingly accept the situation into which God has placed them, and be content to serve Him there.

B. The Practice Re-examined

However you were saved, and whatever condition you find yourself in, you should be willing to remain. It is by the sovereignty of God that you are where you are, and you should not try to change His purpose for you. God has you there for a reason. Conversion is no signal for a person to leave his occupation, his spouse, or even to rush into marriage. God allows you to be where you are and to stay where you are for a purpose. If you have recently come to Christ or have been a Christian for some time, and you are wondering why God has you where you are, don't dwell on your situation; concentrate on spiritual service and obedience to Christ. Let God change the social structure through your righteous life-style.

Focusing on the Facts

1. What specific issues did the apostle Paul address in 1 Corinthians 7:17-24 (see p. 66)?
2. What is the overall context of 1 Corinthians 7 (see p. 66)?
3. What two groups were pressuring the Corinthian believers concerning singleness and marriage, and what were their philosophies (see pp. 66-67)?
4. What is the overarching principle concerning Christians and their response to the social structure in which they live (see p. 67)?
5. The Christian life is not _____ but _____ (see p. 67).
6. What kind of attitude could have destroyed the Corinthian church (see p. 68)?
7. True or false: When Christianity becomes closely identified with a social movement, the message of the gospel is in danger of being lost (see p. 68).
8. Are Christians disqualified from involvement in social causes? Explain your answer (see p. 68).
9. Explain Christianity's role in social reform throughout history (see p. 69).
10. Should Christians overthrow ungodly governments? Support your answer from Scripture (see p. 69).
11. What did the Jewish leaders of Jesus' day think the Messiah would do when He appeared on earth (see p. 71)?

12. What does Paul mean when he uses the term *called* in verses 17-24 (see pp. 71-72)?
13. Describe the historical background of uncircumcision and the reason for it (see p. 72).
14. What was the difference between the circumcision controversy of Corinth and Galatia (see p. 73)?
15. _____ is the only mark of faithfulness the Lord recognizes (p. 73).
16. Is it wrong for a Christian to seek promotion in a job or business? Explain your answer (see p. 74).
17. Must a slave who receives Christ continue in his slavery? Support your answer biblically (see pp. 74-75).
18. What is Paul's advice to those who had the opportunity to be free (1 Cor. 7:21; see p. 75)?
19. Explain Paul's appeal to Philemon concerning Onesimus (see p. 76).
20. Explain what Paul meant when he said that a free man is Christ's servant and a slave is the Lord's freeman (see pp. 76-77).
21. What was the price involved in setting men free from the penalty of sin (1 Pet. 1:18-19; see p. 77)?
22. What is your responsibility as a Christian in your present social state (see p. 78)?

Pondering the Principles

1. The first principle we learned is that Christianity does not promote revolution. Since the Lord has sovereignly called each person to salvation within their prospective social status, we should not focus on changing our status. The first illustration given by Paul was that of Jew and Gentile. He explained that if you were Jewish and circumcised when you came to Christ, you were not to become uncircumcised. Likewise, if you were a Gentile, you were not to seek circumcision. The issue is not circumcision but keeping the commandments of God (v. 19). If you are a believer, do not seek to reform your government because it isn't treating you fairly. Concentrate on the internal—your spiritual life—not the external. Read over the lesson again and ask God to right any wrong motives you might have concerning your attitude toward government.

2. Another lesson we learned is that Christianity is not social resistance or rebellion. The only reason for civil disobedience toward the government is when you are commanded to do something that is expressly forbidden in Scripture (cf. Acts

4:18-20). God's command in 1 Corinthians 7:17-24 is to obey the social structure in which you find yourself, whether it be democratic or totalitarian. Study the following passages and write down each command: Romans 13:1-7; 1 Timothy 2:1-4; 1 Peter 2:13-15; and Titus 3:1-2.

5
Reasons for Remaining Single—Part 1

Outline

Introduction
A. The Biblical Basis for Marriage
  1. The grace of marriage
  2. The picture of marriage
  3. The institution of marriage
B. The Biblical Basis for Singleness
  1. Singleness is good
  2. Singleness is a gift
  3. Singleness is not related to salvation

Lesson
I. The Pressure of the System (vv. 25-27)
  A. The Audience (v. 25a)
  B. The Authority (v.25b)
    1. Paul's conviction
    2. Paul's character
  C. The Antagonism (v. 26)
    1. The Christian's conflict
    2. The Christian's choice
      a) The problem
      b) The prediction
      c) The persecution
  D. The Absolute (v. 27)
    1. The married
    2. The unmarried
II. The Problems of the Flesh (v. 28)
  A. The Problems Identified
  B. The Problems Illustrated
    1. "Trouble"
    2. "Flesh"
III. The Passing of the World (vv. 29-31)

A. The Forsaking of Worldly Things
   1. The temporary factor
   2. The time factor
B. The Futility of Worldly Things
   1. Marriage
   2. Emotions
   3. Possessions
   4. Pleasure

Introduction

In 1 Corinthians 7, the apostle Paul deals with problems surrounding the issue of marriage. But specifically in verses 25-31, he gives six reasons for remaining single. In his discussion of marriage and singleness, Paul has made it clear that neither state is spiritually better than the other. Spirituality is not based on your marital status but on your obedience to God.

A. The Biblical Basis for Marriage

Throughout the seventh chapter, Paul has shown a balanced approach toward the issue of singleness and marriage. The Bible gives a balanced view in the area of marriage, and it recognizes that for whom the Lord wills, singleness is better than marriage. The church needs to maintain a balance in understanding this most important issue. To better understand the balance between singleness and marriage, we need to see other passages in the Bible that emphasize the reality of marriage.

1. The grace of marriage

The apostle Peter called marriage "the grace of life" in 1 Peter 3:7: "In like manner, ye husbands, dwell with them according to knowledge, giving honor unto the wife as unto the weaker vessel, and as being heirs together of the grace of life."

2. The picture of marriage

In Ephesians 5:22-32, the apostle Paul describes marriage as the picture of Christ's relationship to the church. He said, "Wives, submit yourselves unto your own husbands, as unto the Lord. For the husband is the head of the wife, even as Christ is the head of the church; and he is the savior of the body. Therefore, as the church is subject unto Christ, so let the wives be to their own husbands in everything" (vv. 22-24).

3. The institution of marriage

   In Matthew 19:4-6, the Lord Himself acknowledges that marriage is a sacred and holy thing instituted by God. He said, "Have ye not read that he who made them at the beginning, made them male and female; and said, For this cause shall a man leave father and mother, and shall cleave to his wife, and they two shall be one flesh? Wherefore, they are no more two, but one flesh. What therefore God hath joined together, let not man put asunder."

B. The Biblical Basis for Singleness

   While recognizing the normalcy of marriage, the Bible also recognizes singleness as an option for the Christian. Many books, conferences, and programs today focus on the biblical standards for marriage and the family. While many of those are helpful, much less attention is given to what the Bible says about singleness. A great deal of contemporary literature and programs for singles are directed toward helping them "endure" while they wait for marriage. That seems to reflect an underlying assumption that being single is not quite normal and is certainly not desirable.

   As soon as our daughters reach the age of twenty to twenty-two, we begin to panic if they don't have marriage in sight. And if our sons are twenty to twenty-five and aren't married, we begin to wonder if they have a secret problem that we don't know about. Often the pressure of those kinds of worries produce marriages that turn out to be disastrous. Such marriages may be more the will of the parents than the will of God. The first thing a father and mother can do in such a situation is to consider whether God has designed their child to be single. The Bible teaches a balanced approach concerning the possibility of remaining single. First Corinthians 7 gives three basic principles concerning the decision regarding singleness.

   1. Singleness is good

      In 1 Corinthians 7:1 Paul says, "It is good for a man not to touch a woman." We've learned that the phrase *to touch a woman* means to have a sexual relationship. Paul is emphasizing that it is good for a man to remain single and not to marry.

   2. Singleness is a gift

      Paul says in verse 7 that "every man hath his proper gift

of God, one after this manner, and another after that." God gifts certain people with singleness. It's not that they cannot find someone to marry; it's that they do not choose to marry because God has enabled them to withstand sexual desire for the sake of advancing His kingdom through undivided service. Remaining single for them is a gift from God.

3.   Singleness is not related to salvation

Your marital status has no relationship to salvation. Your becoming a Christian is not conditioned on whether you are married or single. For example, you should not divorce your spouse once you become saved, thinking you could have a greater devotion to God. That was precisely the conflict in Corinth. The Jewish leaders were saying you had to get married, and the Gentiles were saying you must be celibate. The apostle Paul says in verse 20, "Let every man abide in the same calling in which he was called." You are to remain in whatever state you were saved.

Lesson

Paul writes verses 25-40 to encourage those who have the gift of singleness. Admittedly, many who are single have difficulty because sin alone has brought on their singleness. But the person to whom God has given the gift of singleness has many practical advantages. In an effort to answer all the questions the Corinthians had concerning this issue, Paul gives six reasons for remaining single: (1) the pressure of the system (vv. 25-27), (2) the problems of the flesh (v. 28), (3) the passing of the world (vv. 29-31), (4) the preoccupations of marriage (vv. 32-35), (5) the promises of fathers (vv. 36-38), and (6) the permanency of marriage (vv. 39-40).

I. THE PRESSURE OF THE SYSTEM (vv. 25-27)

"Now concerning virgins, I have no commandment of the Lord; yet I give my judgment, as one that hath obtained mercy of the Lord to be faithful. I suppose, therefore, that this is good for the present distress, I say, that it is good for a man so to be. Art thou bound unto a wife? Seek not to be loosed. Art thou loosed from a wife? Seek not a wife."

A. The Audience (v. 25*a*)

In order to understand the passage, we must understand whom Paul is speaking to. The Greek word Paul uses for "virgin" is *parthenōn*. It refers to someone who is unmarried. The word for "virgin" can be used for men, such as in Revelation 14:4, but here in 1 Corinthians 7:25 it is used with the feminine article denoting single girls. Paul is speaking to virgin daughters who were unmarried.

B. The Authority (v. 25*b*)

Paul says concerning those virgins, "I have no command of the Lord." Again, as in verse 12, Paul points out that Jesus gave no direct teaching on singleness, although He alluded to it in Matthew 19:12. Yet the apostle's teaching is no less divine and authoritative. When the Lord stated a command, Paul quoted it. And when the Lord gave no command while He was on earth, Paul made that clear. In verse 12 Paul says, "To the rest speak I, not the Lord." In other words, "Here's an issue Jesus did not speak on, so I'm going to address it."

1. Paul's conviction

Paul says in verse 25, "I give my judgment." Paul is simply saying there were issues that the Lord Himself addressed and there were some He did not. But when the Lord did not speak about a particular issue, His apostles often did, and it came as though it were straight from Him. Sometimes when the apostles spoke, they gave absolute, authoritative commands, but on other occasions, they gave only guidelines because there could be no absolutes. Paul, in this passage, is giving a guideline for living in the present age. Because all Scripture is inspired by God (2 Tim. 3:16), this is not just Paul's advice but the advice of the Holy Spirit.

2. Paul's character

Paul not only shared his convictions but also lived out the advice he gave. He describes himself as one "that hath obtained mercy of the Lord to be faithful" (v. 25). As an apostle who by the mercy of the Lord was found trustworthy, Paul's conviction was that it is better for single Christians to remain that way, if they have that gift from God. Although this perspective is authoritative, it is not given as an absolute command. It is a guideline—thoroughly dependable advice—and is stated twice in verse 26 as being "good." When he says later in verse 40, "I

85

think also that I have the Spirit of God," he is not saying he is not sure; he is being sarcastic with those in the congregation who acted as if they alone had the mind of the Spirit.

By the phrase "one that hath obtained mercy of the Lord to be faithful," he is saying, "You can trust my judgment." Paul, by God's grace, had been given unusual insights into the truth. The Corinthians could trust what he had to say. Paul felt indebted to the mercy of Christ for the truths he had gained. Christ, by His grace, made him an authoritative apostle.

C. The Antagonism (v. 26)

Paul says, "I suppose, therefore, that this is good for the present distress" (v. 26). The phrase "I suppose" is somewhat misleading. The Greek word is *nomizō*, which means "I hold" or "I consider." This is not a guess for Paul but a conviction.

1. The Christian's conflict

The first reason Paul gives for remaining single is the pressure of the system. The Greek word for "distress" is *anankē*, which means "stress," "calamity," or "the means of calamity" (such as torture or violence, as in Luke 21:23 and 2 Cor. 6:4). Some have suggested this refers to the violent conflict between the new creation in Christ and the world system. When a person becomes a Christian, he immediately gets into some degree of conflict with the ungodly system around him. Paul is saying here that it is difficult to be married because of the distress and violence of Satan's evil system.

Persecution is difficult enough for a single person, but the problems and pain are multiplied for one who is married. If Paul had been married, his suffering would have been magnified. He would be worried about his family and know that they were worried about him. They would have suffered every time he was beaten, stoned, and imprisoned and would have been constantly fearful for his life. Who would have taken care of them in his absence? Who would have taught his children and comforted his wife? His suffering and his practical problems would have increased and the effectiveness of his ministry decreased. Married believers who go through social turmoil and persecution cannot escape carrying a much heavier load than those who are single.

2. The Christian's choice

Paul ends verse 26 by stating, "I say, that it is good for a man so to be." Paul is saying, "I hold the conviction that it is good for a man to remain unmarried." He has already stated his conviction concerning singleness in verses 1 and 8 of this chapter.

a) The problem

Marriage was a major encumbrance to anyone who was a Christian in Paul's time. Because of the impending violence, Christians could expect to receive persecution that would not only affect them but their families as well. Paul knew wholesale persecution was inevitable. He knew of the heartbreaking losses that could come to those who have a family.

b) The prediction

Paul was aware of imminent persecution. In the first place, Jesus had predicted it. In John 15:18-19 our Lord says, "If the world hate you, ye know that it hated me before it hated you. If ye were of the world, the world would love its own; but because ye are not of the world, but I have chosen you out of the world, therefore the world hateth you." Jesus had warned the disciples that they would be made outcasts from the synagogue and said, "An hour is coming for everyone who kills you to think that he is offering service to God" (John 16:2, NASB).

c) The persecution

Paul seemed to sense the coming terrible Roman persecutions, the first of which would begin under Nero some ten years after Paul wrote 1 Corinthians. Nero refined torture to a diabolical art, and his name became synonymous with sadistic cruelty. He had Christians sewn up in animal skins and thrown before wild dogs to be torn apart and eaten. Other believers were dressed in clothes soaked in wax, tied to trees, and set on fire—becoming human candles for his garden parties (cf. 1 Pet. 4:12). Corinth would furnish one of the early Christian martyrs. *Foxe's Book of Martyrs*, tells us that Erastus, the treasurer of

Corinth (Rom. 16:23) and probably a convert of Paul's, was martyred.

D. The Absolute (v. 27)

Paul had been talking about those who were unmarried. Now he addresses those who were already married. He says, "Art thou bound unto a wife? Seek not to be loosed. Art thou loosed from a wife? Seek not a wife" (v. 27).

1. The married

The apostle Paul gives an absolute command here in verse 27. He is saying if you are already married, do not divorce your spouse. He just said in verse 10, "Let not the wife depart from her husband." Whatever the distress, those who are already married must endure it.

2. The unmarried

For those who have the gift of singleness, it is much wiser to remain single. Paul says, "Art thou loosed from a wife? Seek not a wife" (v. 27). Paul is saying to cherish our singleness as a blessing from God and take advantage of it. Keep in mind that Paul is talking about those who have the gift of singleness. Many might be wondering how this passage applies to today, with the general lack of persecution against Christianity. However, many signs point to times of increasing conflict and even persecution for Christians in our world.

In Matthew 24 Jesus vividly pictures the turmoil and terror of the end times. It will be characterized by wars, apostasy, persecution, false prophets, and universal tribulation. We can already see overpopulation, pollution, rampant crime, and immorality, as well as false prophets, cults, and increased threats of global war. Paul was right on target when he told Timothy, "Evil men and seducers shall become worse and worse, deceiving, and being deceived" (2 Tim. 3:13). The turn of the century could produce widespread warfare, civil strife, revolution, famine, disease, persecution, despotism, natural disasters, economic stagnation, and depression.

Being married will only complicate your life at that time because of the problem of caring for your spouse and children. From the time Jesus first arrived on earth until the day He returns, many pressures confront the Christian. We are to anticipate suffering and the hatred of the world. If you have the gift of singleness and you don't burn with sexual desire, be content. The nearer you get to the end of time, the higher the price you'll pay for your faith.

II. THE PROBLEMS OF THE FLESH (v. 28)

"But and if thou marry, thou hast not sinned; and if a virgin marry, she hath not sinned. Nevertheless, such shall have trouble in the flesh; but I spare you."

A. The Problems Identified

Paul again wants to make it clear that it is not a sin for single believers to get married, as long as it is to another believer (v. 39; cf. 2 Cor. 6:14). Even those with the gift of singleness do not sin if they get married. So if you should marry, you have not sinned. The point is that marriage is a legitimate option, but it is good to consider first the option of singleness. Paul recognizes that marriage is still the option of the majority according to God's design. But he also recognizes the distinct probability that those who do marry will have trouble in this life.

B. The Problems Illustrated

What does Paul mean when he says, "Such shall have trouble in the flesh" (v. 28)? The apostle Paul is giving practical advice, not a moral or spiritual command. He is describing the problems that a married couple will face as believers in Christ.

1. "Trouble"

The Greek word for "trouble" is *thlipsis*, which means "pressed together" or "under pressure." Believers are still sinful and subject to limitations in the flesh. It is hard enough for a sinner to live with himself, let alone with another sinner. That is where the trouble comes. When two people are bound together in marriage, the problems of human nature are multiplied. Add to that the children who will be produced. Children of Christian parents are born sinful, as are all children, and they do not become sinless when they are saved. They will have some measure of conflict with each other and with their parents.

2. "Flesh"

Paul uses the Greek word *sarx* for "flesh." It refers to the lower nature of man. Even though the Holy Spirit desires us to experience perfect unity, our humanness creates problems in the marriage relationship. Marriage involves two distinct people with two distinct personalities, characteristics, emotions, temperaments, and wills. Each partner has some degree of anger, selfishness, dishonesty, pride, forgetfulness, and thoughtlessness. That is true even of the best of marriages. If God has given you the gift of singleness, it is good to stay that way to avoid the problems that our humanness brings into marriage.

Marriage should not be looked upon as merely a way of escape from sexual problems. Loneliness, sexual temptation, lust, and immorality are not eradicated once you've found a marriage partner. In fact, many times, if there have been problems in one's past, simply marrying will not change those problems. Many people carry their loneliness right into marriage and end up making the other person lonely as well. And although it is God's design for normal sexual fulfillment, marriage does not end the temptations of lust or immorality. If there have been problems with those things in the past, the mind may be drawn to illicit fulfillment outside the marriage relationship. Sexual sins will not be corrected by marriage. They may even be worsened by the person who has not correctly dealt with his past problems.

Marriage is not the solution to all problems. It is the right course of action for one reason only: fulfilling the will of God. If He wants you married, then marry the right person, but only if that's clearly God's will. If you are confident you have the gift of singleness, you will avoid the special problems of the flesh that come with marriage, as well as the pressure of the system.

III. THE PASSING OF THE WORLD (vv. 29-31)

"But this I say, brethren, The time is short; it remaineth that both they that have wives be as though they had none; and they that weep, as though they wept not; and they that rejoice, as though they rejoiced not; and they that buy, as though they possessed not; and they that use this world, as not abusing it; for the fashion of this world passeth away."

A. The Forsaking of Worldly Things

1. The temporary factor

The focal point of this portion of Scripture is verse 31: "The fashion of this world passeth away." Paul is saying that marriage is part of what will pass away with the world. The Greek word for "form" is *schēma* and it refers to "a manner of life, a way of doing things, or mode of existence." Although God ordained and blessed marriage, it is not eternal (Matt. 22:30). Godly marriages are "made in heaven," but they will not carry over into heaven. Paul is saying marriage is part of what is passing away. It is designed for this life only and will disappear with this world. That thought bothers many people because they assume that when they marry, they will always be married. But marriage is not an eternal commodity.

2. The time factor

Paul begins verse 29 by saying, "This I say, brethren, The time is short" or, literally, "The time has been shortened." The Greek word for "time" is *kairos*. It refers to a fixed, definite period of time. God has set an appointed time for things in this world to be accomplished. The time God has allotted to this world is brief. James says, "Ye know not what shall be on the next day. For what is your life? It is even a vapor that appeareth for a little time, and then vanisheth away" (James 4:14). Your life is a flickering candle that is gone with the first breath of God's divine wind. First Peter cites Isaiah 40:6-7: "All flesh is like grass, and all the glory of man like the flower of grass" (1:24; cf. James 1:10).

B. The Futility of Worldly Things

Paul gives four examples of the Christian's freedom from attachment to the world in verses 29-31:

1. Marriage

Marriage is a part of the world's passing system. And if you have a gift for singleness, realize that marriage is something with which you may not want to involve yourself. It is God's design that we have a light attachment to earthly things. Paul ends verse 29 by saying, "It remaineth that both they that have wives be as though they had none." Paul is saying that because of the brevity of time, you should above all things concentrate on what is eternal and not temporal. That does not mean you are to neglect your spouse for the sake of the ministry. It does mean, however, that you are to fulfill your responsibilities both to your spouse *and* the Lord. A brief life and hard circumstances do not lessen the obligations of husbands and wives (cf. Eph. 5:22-33; Col. 3:18-19). Paul is teaching that marriage should not reduce a Christian's obligation and devotion to the Lord and His work. Whether you have been gifted for singleness or marriage is not the main issue. Your responsibility is to devote your entire life to the Lord in whatever state you're in. The responsibilities of marriage are no excuse for ignoring the Lord's work.

It has become increasingly difficult for Christians—including missionaries—to be strongly dedicated to serving the Lord. In many cases they do not want to be separated from the companionship of their wives for more than a week or two at most, even though important ministry needs may take more time than that. The focus of all Christians, whether married or single, should be "on the things above, not on the things that are on the earth" (Col. 3:2, NASB). First John 2:15, 17 says, "Love not the world, neither the things that are in the world. If any man love the world, the love of the Father is not in him. . . . And the world passeth away, and the lust of it; but he that doeth the will of God abideth forever." You can love your wife and at the same time keep your priorities for God in proper perspective.

2. Emotions

Paul deals with the area of human emotions in verse 30: "And they that weep, as though they wept not." Emotions for the most part are not uncontrollable. Christians are not to be emotionless and certainly not hard-hearted or indifferent. But Christian love is much more than emotion; it is an act of the will. Our emotions should not rise or fall simply as a result of our circumstances. True love will, in fact, stabilize our emotions when it is kept in the proper spiritual perspective. When a relative or loved one dies or becomes handicapped or diseased, it is not the time to laugh or celebrate. On the other hand, the mature Christian does not lose all hope, purpose, or motivation for living.

The apostle Paul also says, "And they that rejoice, as though they rejoiced not" (v. 30). The Christian must also learn not to be carried away with rejoicing over things that will ultimately pass away. Don't become overjoyed with what makes the world happy. Many times our own successes or accomplishments excite us more than spiritual victory. Even when we give the Lord credit for the blessings we receive, we can easily lose our perspective and be controlled more by our emotions than by good judgment and spiritual priorities.

3. Possessions

Paul also says, "And they that buy, as though they possessed not." The accumulation of money and of the things it can buy is the preoccupation of many Christians. But when that occurs, it is hard to distinguish them from the world. Paul in effect is saying, "Be in the world, but not of it." Tie loosely to the world and its relationships, emotions, and commodities. Many times, Christians are more preoccupied with their bank account than their spiritual life. We're more worried about how to decorate our house or how expensive our cars are than spiritual realities and eternal truths. Christians should be predominately concerned with that which is inward and spiritual rather than that which is outward and material.

4. Pleasure

Paul finishes the list in verse 31: "And they that use this world, as not abusing it; for the fashion of this world passeth away." The Scriptures emphasize that the Christian is to promote peace, but many times peace is mistaken for pleasure. Especially in times of affluence, permissiveness, and inordinate self-acceptance, it is easy to strive for pleasure rather than peace. And pleasures that are not immoral or extravagant in and of themselves may still be worldly—and dangerous to your spiritual life. Inordinate leisure time, early retirement, and more comfortable homes can so dominate our minds that we can begin to neglect the spiritual area of our lives. So many simply live to have a good time rather than giving the glory to God. We can become so busy enjoying things in the world that we disqualify ourselves from being useful to Him. We should focus our entire life on things of eternal consequence.

Many have wondered what Paul means in verse 31 when he says, "And they that use this world, as not abusing it." Paul is encouraging believers not to overdo their identification with the world. Be happy, enjoy your marriage, love your wife, and give of yourselves to one another, but don't let your surroundings become all-inclusive. Marriage, sorrow, rejoicing, possessions, and pleasure all have their proper place in the Christian life. But those things become sinful when they dominate our thoughts and behavior. Don't overvalue earthly things. Keep them in perspective.

Paul's entire point is that it is much easier in this life to remain single. You would not have the preoccupation with marriage and family and consequently you would not have the potential sorrow of the death of a loved one. If you have the gift of singleness, use it for God's glory. If you do not have the gift or are already married, concentrate on spiritual service more so than present earthly pleasure.

Focusing on the Facts

1. What three passages give a good, biblical basis for marriage (see pp. 82-83)?
2. Does the Bible give a scriptural basis for singleness? Explain your answer with Scripture (see pp. 83-84).
3. What three basic principles regarding singleness can be found in 1 Corinthians 7 (see pp. 83-84)?
4. What six reasons does Paul give for remaining single in 1 Corinthians 7:25-40 (see p. 84)?
5. What is meant by the term *virgin* in verse 25 (see p. 85)?
6. What was Paul's conviction concerning the issue of singleness (see p. 85)?
7. What was the basis for Paul's conviction (see p. 85)?
8. Describe what is meant by remaining single because of the pressure of the system (see pp. 86-87).
9. Why is persecution compounded for someone who is married as opposed to someone who isn't (see p. 86)?
10. Describe the Roman persecutions under Nero and their result (see p. 87).
11. What was Paul's advice to those who were already married (v. 27; see p. 88)?
12. Explain the potential problems in today's society that would make the decision easier for remaining single (see pp. 88-89).
13. For the Christian, the _____ you get to the end of time, the _____ the _____ you'll pay for your faith (see p. 89).
14. Describe the second reason Paul gives for remaining single. Why is it hard for two people who are married to live together (see pp. 89-90)?
15. True or false: Marriage should be looked upon as a way of escape from sexual problems. Explain your answer (see p. 90).

16. What is the sole reason for marrying (see p. 90)?
17. Explain the reason Paul gives in verses 29-31 for remaining single (see pp. 90-91)?
18. What four examples does Paul give to explain the Christian's freedom from attachment to the world (see pp. 91-92)?
19. Explain the balance between the responsibilities of a person in his marriage and his relationship to God (see pp. 91-92).
20. How is a Christian supposed to deal with his emotions (see pp. 92-93)?
21. What is to be the Christian's attitude toward his earthly possessions (see p. 93)?
22. Christians should be predominately concerned with that which is _____ and _____ rather than that which is _____ and _____ (see p. 93).
23. Are Christians supposed to seek pleasure? Explain your answer (see p. 93).
24. True or false: Paul's point in 1 Corinthians 7:25-31 is that it is much easier in this life to remain single (see p. 94).
25. If you do not have the gift of singleness or are already married, concentrate on _____ _____ more so than _____ _____ (see p. 94).

Pondering the Principles

1. In 1 Corinthians 7:25-31, Paul first addresses those who have never been married. His conviction was that they should seriously consider the possibility of remaining single because of the conflict with the world's sinful system. Paul did not lay down an absolute command but gave an authoritative guideline. Are you presently struggling with your singleness? If you are, would you seriously consider remaining single based on the apostle Paul's strong conviction? With the potential problems facing our world, it may very well be that married believers will go through much more anguish and persecution than those who are single. Ask God to confirm in your heart whether He would rather you be single or married.

2. Paul realized the difficulty of being married to another sinful human being. When two people are bound together in marriage, the problems of our sinful human nature are multiplied. Within marriage, you have two distinct personalities, emotions, temperaments, and wills. As a result, it was the conviction of the apostle Paul that it was better to remain single. As a married person, don't expect things to be perfect just because you and your

spouse are Christians. As a single person, realize what is involved in marriage and then ask the Lord for guidance in choosing whether to remain single. Remember, it is not a sin for single believers to be married, as long as it is to another believer. Even those with the gift of singleness do not sin if they get married. The point is that marriage is a legitimate option, but it is good to consider first the option of singleness. Reread the chapter, noting the reasons for remaining single and ask for wisdom. If you are married, seek to walk in obedience and be the best spouse you can be.

3. Paul emphasized that marriage is only for this life and not for eternity. He then gave four examples of temporal things that could lead to an inordinate attachment to the world: marriage, emotions, possessions, and pleasure. How is your spiritual experience in relation to those areas? Do you find yourself more concerned with your wife than Christ? How about your finances? In reality, is your bank account more important than your spiritual life? If so, take each of the four areas: marriage, emotions, possessions, and pleasure and for the next four days, single out one and ask God to search your heart to reveal the real motives in your thoughts and behavior.

6
Reasons for Remaining Single—Part 2

Outline

Introduction
A. The Design of Marriage
B. The Decision of Singleness
   1. The implication
   2. The importance

Review
  I. The Pressure of the System (vv. 26-28)
 II. The Problems of the Flesh (v. 28)
III. The Passing of the World (vv. 29-31)

Lesson
IV. The Preoccupations of Marriage (vv. 32-35)
   A. Divided Interests (vv. 32-33)
     1. A carefree attitude
     2. A confident assertion
       a) Luke 14:17, 20
       b) 1 Corinthians 7:28
   B. Devoted Interests (v. 34)
     1. Holiness
     2. Harmony
   C. Distracted Interests (v. 35)
     1. The negative example of Martha
     2. The positive example of Rachel Saint
 V. The Promises of Fathers (vv. 36-38)
   A. Old Testament Culture
     1. The guardian
       a) Genesis 24:1-4
       b) Genesis 21:21
       c) Genesis 38:6
     2. The government
       a) Genesis 41:45

Introduction

A. The Design of Marriage

In the previous chapter, we studied several reasons for remaining single. It must be emphasized, however, that for the majority, marriage will be the norm. It is the relationship that God has designed for most people, and it is a sacred and holy thing.

1. Its stability

The Bible is replete with passages extolling the virtues of marriage. The apostle Paul in 1 Corinthians 7 says, "Let every man have his own wife, and let every woman have her own husband" (v. 2).

2. Its significance

Proverbs 18:22 says, "Whoso findeth a wife findeth a good thing." God looks on marriage with absolute favor and extols it as a good thing.

3. Its standard

Jeremiah 29:6 says, "Take to yourselves wives, and beget sons and daughters . . . and give your daughters to husbands, that they may bear sons and daughters, that ye may be increased there, and not diminished." Although that was commanded by the Lord while the Israelites were in captivity, the general principle is for God's people to marry and procreate. Marriage is God's standard for the majority.

4. Its sacredness

In 1 Timothy 4:2-3 Paul explains that in the last days heretics will deny the Lord, "speaking lies in hypocrisy, having their conscience seared with a hot iron, forbidding to marry." According to the apostle Paul, that is heresy. Marriage is acceptable to God.

5. Its satisfaction

Hebrews 13:4 says, "Marriage is honorable in all, and the bed undefiled." God looks very favorably on marriage.

B. The Decision of Singleness

1. The implication

Marriage, however, is not the norm for everyone. God has given some the special gift of remaining single. They, unlike others, do not need to be married to fulfill God's will. They are, in fact, fulfilling God's will to its fullest when they remain single. The church has tended to categorize single people as abnormal, but God has specifically designed singleness for some. Paul's conviction was clearly articulated in 1 Corinthians 7:7: "I would that all men were even as myself. But every man hath his proper gift of God, one after this manner, and another after that." Paul is calling those who have the gift of singleness to remain that way. Those who don't have the gift are to marry. Some are gifted for marriage and some for singleness.

Singleness is a special gift of God. Single people do not need to be looked upon as if they are strange or abnormal. They are just as qualified for spiritual service as one who is married. Marriage is designed by God to complete two individuals who would otherwise be incomplete. But single people have been gifted by God to such a capacity that they may be the most complete of all. They are uniquely designed by God to function within the body of Christ, without the need for a mate.

2. The importance

Jewish leaders in Corinth were saying you had to be

married. Greek philosophers were saying you could be more devoted to God by being single. The apostle Paul countered that by saying marriage and singleness aren't even the issue—spirituality is. He says in verse 20, "Let every man abide in the same calling in which he was called." Again in verse 24 he says, "Let every man in whatever state he is called, there abide with God." As if the reader were not paying attention, Paul says for the third time in verse 27, "Art thou bound unto a wife? Seek not to be loosed. Art thou loosed from a wife? Seek not a wife." The issue is not a person's marital status but his spirituality. Neither is inherently better; God designs some for singleness and others for marriage.

Paul realized that those with the gift of singleness were going to be under tremendous pressure to be married. Society accepts marriage as the standard, and many times single people tend to be pressured into getting married. The pressure may begin with Mom and Dad and move to peer pressure from nearly everyone else. Many church activities have family orientations and tend to leave out activities for the single person. The church must recognize that God has gifted some people for singleness and some for marriage. Neither is less significant than the other; they are simply different in His divine plan.

Review

In 1 Corinthians 7:25-40, Paul gives six reasons for remaining single. For those who have the gift of singleness, Paul is giving encouragement to stay that way.

I. THE PRESSURE OF THE SYSTEM (vv. 26-28; see pp. 84-89)

Paul says in verse 26 that those who are married will encounter pressure from the world: "I suppose, therefore, that this is good for the present distress, I say, that it is good for a man so to be." Paul realized that persecution was coming under the harsh rule of the Roman empire and wanted to prepare the Corinthians for it. He was acknowledging that for those who were married, persecution would be far worse on them emotionally. Wives would be likely to face the death of their husbands and children the death of their parents. Family ties make the pain and anguish all the greater in times of persecution. If you have the gift of singleness, you won't have that pressure to the same degree should persecution befall you.

II. THE PROBLEMS OF THE FLESH (v. 28; see pp. 89-90)

The second reason for remaining single is the problems of the flesh. In the middle of verse 28 Paul says, "Nevertheless, such shall have trouble in the flesh; but I spare you." It is not wrong to marry, but the apostle Paul wants you to know that you will have trouble in this life. Marriage frequently intensifies human weaknesses. You first have to deal with issues in your home and then in the world around you. It adds friction to living. Marriage is wonderful when it occurs the way God designed it, but make no mistake about it, there still will be times of great difficulty.

III. THE PASSING OF THE WORLD (vv. 29-31; see pp. 90-94)

In the last chapter, we saw another reason for remaining single: the passing of the world. Verses 29-31 say, "This I say, brethren, The time is short; it remaineth that both they that have wives be as though they had none; and they that weep, as though they wept not; and they that rejoice, as though they rejoiced not; and they that buy, as though they possessed not; and they that use this world, as not abusing it; for the fashion of this world passeth away." Marriage is only a part of this world and will not occupy a place in heaven.

According to the apostle Paul, a single person is more easily detached from the world's relationships, emotions, pleasures, and commodities. A Christian, whether single or married, is to set his affections on things above (Col. 3:2). It is not wrong to have pleasure, purchase things, be emotional, or be married. Paul is simply saying that those things are wrong when they divert our attention from serving Christ. They become an attachment to the passing world.

When you marry, you will probably buy life insurance so that if you die suddenly, your children will be taken care of. You have to save money for their future education as well. You also have to buy medical insurance for your family's physical needs. When your family grows, you buy a bigger house and a bigger car. You also have to be sensitive to the psychological, emotional, and spiritual needs of your family. Paul is saying that there is much involved in being married that a single person could do well to avoid. If you have the gift of singleness and don't need to involve yourself in a marriage relationship, Paul's advice is that you are better off remaining single.

Lesson

IV. THE PREOCCUPATIONS OF MARRIAGE (vv. 32-35)

"I would have you without care. He that is unmarried careth for the things that belong to the Lord, how he may please the Lord; but he that is married careth for the things that are of the world, how he may please his wife. There is a difference also between a wife and a virgin. The unmarried woman careth for the things of the Lord, that she may be holy both in body and in spirit; but she that is married careth for the things of the world, how she may please her husband. And this I speak for your own profit; not that I may cast a snare upon you, but for that which is seemly, and that ye may attend upon the Lord without distraction."

A. Divided Interests (vv. 32-33)

According to the apostle Paul, those who are married need to be preoccupied with each other. He says in verses 32-33, "He that is unmarried careth for the things that belong to the Lord. . . . But he that is married careth for the things that are of the world, how he may please his wife." Verse 33 should end, "His interests are divided." The best manuscripts contain this last portion. Both husbands and wives are concerned about the earthly needs of each other—as they should be. But one who is unmarried has the opportunity to be undivided in his devotion to the Lord.

1. A carefree attitude

Paul begins verse 32 by saying, "I would have you without care." He was trying to free the Corinthians of the anxiety that marriage would cause. Paul is saying, "I'd like you to have a carefree attitude about serving the Lord." J. B. Lightfoot, commenting on this verse, says that a man who is a hero in himself becomes a coward when he thinks of his widowed wife and his orphaned children.

2. A confident assertion

There are certain cares that encumber your mind when you're married. Paul says, "He that is married careth for the things that are of the world, how he may please his wife" (v. 33). A single person, however, "careth for the things that belong to the Lord, how he may please the Lord" (v. 32). The apostle is not saying that all single people are totally devoted to Jesus Christ. He is simply saying that the single person has the potential for that kind of devotion. He has but one set of cares: his own. The married person, on the other hand, has a divided set of cares: the Lord and his family. It isn't that those divided interests are bad; they're good and they're both designed by God. However, there is in marriage the inability for single-mindedness. Several passages speak to this issue.

a) Luke 14:17, 20—In the parable of the great supper, Jesus says, "Come; for all things are now ready" (v. 17). However, one man replied, "I have married a wife, and, therefore, I cannot come" (v. 20). I wonder how many times in the history of the church there have been ministry opportunities open, but someone married and didn't go. It isn't wrong to marry, but maybe it would be better to remain single.

b) 1 Corinthians 7:28—Paul said, "If thou marry, thou hast not sinned; and if a virgin marry, she hath not sinned." It is interesting to note that the gift of singleness is the only spiritual gift in Scripture that you have an option to use. Paul is saying to use it. But if you do not use it, you have not sinned. God never makes marriage a sin, unless of course it is to an unbeliever. It may be that God could have used a man and a woman differently if they had remained single, but He will also use them in their marriage.

B. Devoted Interests (v. 34)

The first part of verse 34, "There is a difference also between a wife and a virgin," does not appear in the better manuscripts. The verse should read, "The woman who is unmarried, and the virgin, is concerned about the things of the Lord, that she may be holy both in body and spirit; but one who is married is concerned about the things of the world, how she may please her husband" (NASB). Paul is reiterating that there is a dividedness for those who are married. It isn't wrong to be married; the dividedness is simply a fact. A single person, male or female, has the potential of a concentrated devotion to the Lord. A married person, however, must along with his devotion to Christ care for his family. That is what Paul means when he says in verse 35, "Ye may attend upon the Lord without distraction."

A single person need not have any distraction from serving the Lord. How many times have you heard of a believer struggling to please his or her unbelieving partner and the

Lord? What about someone who is married to a Christian who is in sin and tries to live a devoted life—struggling not to fall into sin themselves? You may even have a partner whose dedication to the Lord is outstanding and yet you are still limited in what you can do with the time you have.

1. Holiness

   Paul says at the end of verse 34, "That she may be holy both in body and in spirit." The word *holy* basically means "separated." It is contrasted here with being divided. Paul is not saying single people are more holy than married people. Holiness is not based on your marital status but on the righteousness of God imputed to you. There are many single people who aren't holy and, likewise, there are many married people who are. What the verse is saying is that the person who is not married can be separated unto God both spiritually *and* physically. He has no need to satisfy his sexual desires. And that makes for less spiritual encumbrances as well because he can concentrate fully on his relationship with Christ. The single person, then, has a certain liberty in serving the Lord.

2. Harmony

   The married person need not have divided spiritual loyalties. But practically, the unmarried person, both in body and spirit, is potentially able to set himself apart from the things of this life more exclusively for the Lord's work. Married Christians should not feel guilty about being married, and unmarried Christians should not feel guilty about getting married. The apostle is not trying to add to the burdens and cares that married persons already have, and he is not trying to force single believers into the permanent mold of singleness. Paul's conviction is only for those who have the gift of singleness. He clearly says in 1 Timothy 5:14, "I will, therefore, that the younger women marry." He recognized the innate need for most young women to marry. If you put an undue burden to remain single on those who never had God's gift to remain single, many will have problems. But those who do have the gift should remain single, for there is greater potential for service and devotion to the Lord.

C. Distracted Interests (v. 35)

Paul adds verse 35 to avoid confusion: "This I speak for your own profit; not that I may cast a snare upon you." Paul was not creating a legalistic noose (the literal meaning of the word *snare*); he simply wanted those with the gift of singleness to know "that which is seemly, and that ye may attend upon the Lord without distraction." It isn't that you have to stay single at all cost, even if you have the gift for it. It is not a command; you have the option. Paul is saying, "I'm telling you only for your own good; if you have the gift, you'd be better off using it." The Corinthians were not under compulsion either to marry or to remain single. Paul had two beneficial motives in advising them to remain as they were: He wanted to spare them trouble (vv. 28, 32), and he wanted them to have undistracted devotion to the Lord (v. 35). It must be emphasized, however, that marriage does not prevent great devotion to the Lord, and singleness does not guarantee it. Singleness has fewer hindrances and more advantages. It is easier for a single person to be single-minded in the things of the Lord.

1. The negative example of Martha

Luke 10:38-42 provides a good illustration for those who desire to serve the Lord without distraction: "[Jesus] entered into a certain village; and a certain woman, named Martha, received him into her house. And she had a sister, called Mary, who also sat at Jesus' feet, and heard his word. But Martha was cumbered about much serving, and came to him, and said, Lord, dost thou not care that my sister hath left me to serve alone? Bid her, therefore, that she help me. And Jesus answered, and said unto her, Martha, Martha, thou art anxious and troubled about many things. But one thing is needful, and Mary hath chosen that good part, which shall not be taken away from her."

Jesus was in the home of Mary, Martha, and Lazarus. Jesus sat down and Mary sat at His feet, hanging on His every word. But Martha was busy around the house getting everything ready and serving everyone. There was nothing wrong with preparing the meal; that is biblical hospitality. She simply felt she needed help from her sister, who was doing nothing but sitting at Jesus' feet. She became frustrated and asked Jesus to tell Mary to help her with the serving. Jesus responded by explaining that Mary was doing what she ought to be doing. Mary had a single-minded devotion to the Lord. She was not concerned with the place settings, although those things have their place. It is not wrong to be hospitable, but Martha's preoccupation did cause, in this case, a divided devotion to Christ.

2. The positive example of Rachel Saint

When I was in Quito, Ecuador, I had the wonderful privilege of meeting with Rachel Saint, a single woman who has given her life to discipling the Auca Indians. She is an incredible person. I often think that unmarried people are possibly the most fulfilled people of all because they don't need someone else to make them complete. By the sovereign gift and grace of God, she and many like her are completely devoted to the Lord without encumbrance.

V. THE PROMISES OF FATHERS (vv. 36-38)

"But if any man think that he behaveth himself unseemly toward his virgin, if she pass the flower of her age, and need so require, let him do what he will, he sinneth not; let them marry. Nevertheless, he that standeth steadfast in his heart, having no necessity, but hath power over his own will, and hath so decreed in his heart that he will keep his virgin, doeth well. So, then, he that giveth her in marriage doeth well; but he giveth her not in marriage doeth better."

A. Old Testament Culture

In Jewish culture, parents, and particularly fathers, long had a dominant role in deciding whom their children would marry.

1. The guardian

In the Old Testament, marriages were arranged by the parents.

a) Genesis 24:1-4—Abraham got a wife for Isaac: "Abraham was old, and well stricken in age: and the Lord had blessed Abraham in all things. And Abraham said unto his eldest servant of his house, that ruled over all that he had, Put, I pray thee, thy hand under my thigh; and I will make thee swear by the Lord, the God of heaven, and the God of the earth, that thou shalt not take a wife unto my son of the daughters of the Canaanites, among whom I dwell. But thou shalt go unto my country, and to my kindred, and take a wife unto my son Isaac."

b) Genesis 21:21—Hagar selected a wife for Ishmael: "[Ishmael] dwelt in the wilderness of Paran: and his mother took him a wife out of the land of Egypt."

c) Genesis 38:6—Judah selected a wife for Er: "Judah took a wife for Er, his first-born, whose name was Tamar."

2. The government

There are even instances in the Bible where a king or a priest selected a wife for someone.

a) Genesis 41:45—"Pharaoh called Joseph's name Zaphenathpaneah; and he gave him as his wife Asenath, the daughter of Potiphera, priest of On."

b) 1 Kings 11:19—Another Pharaoh gave a wife to Hadad the Edomite: "Hadad found great favor in the sight of Pharaoh, so that he gave him in marriage the sister of his own wife, the sister of Tahpenes, the queen."

c) 2 Chronicles 24:3—Jehoiada, the high priest, gave two wives to the boy king Joash: "Jehoiada took for him two wives, and he begot sons and daughters."

B. New Testament Culture

Things were much different in New Testament times. Marriage, especially for young people, remained the norm. Paul writes words of instructions to the fathers of those children in verses 36-38, since it was important for them to hear the Holy Spirit's guidelines concerning singleness and marriage. This portion of Scripture, however, is not just a cultural admonition. It contains practical guidelines that speak authoritatively to our day as well.

1. Marriage brokers

History records that around the year 500 B.C., marriage brokers (Heb., *Shadcan*) began appearing. Such brokers were available for consultation on the marriage of your children. You would give one a list of qualifications, and he or she would match your child with a mate.

2. Marriage breakers

The same general custom that prevailed in many ancient societies, such as was seen in the Old and New Testaments, prevailed in Rome also. Some historians credit Rome's decline in part to the weakening of the family caused by the loss of parental control in arranging marriages.

C. Individual Choice

Some feel that in the early history of Israel, the bride and bridegroom had no say in choosing a marriage partner. But as best we can tell from the Scripture, the young man or woman did have something to say about his future spouse. It wasn't just a matter of the father's dogmatic command. Young men had the right to some kind of choice.

1. Proverbs 30:18-19

The writer says, "There are three things which are too wonderful for me, yea, four which I know not: The way of an eagle in the air; the way of a serpent upon a rock; the way of a ship in the midst of the sea; and the way of a man with a maid." The phrase "the way of a man with a maid" may indicate that there was at least some liberty in Hebrew society to pursue a love relationship.

2. Song of Solomon

This Old Testament book expresses the tremendous love between two people. This kind of relationship implies more than just a parental agreement. The context reveals that the will of the man was obviously involved as well as the will of the woman.

3. Genesis 24:57-58

When Abraham's servant asked Rebekah's parents if she could marry Isaac, they said, "We will call the damsel, and inquire at her mouth. And they called Rebekah, and said unto her, Wilt thou go with this man? And she said, I will go." Rebekah had been consulted and made her choice to go with the servant to Isaac.

The father would usually decide on the marriage partner but probably not without the children's involvement in some way. There may have been times when the child's will was overruled, but for the most part their input was considered as a part of the decision.

D. Individual Concern

1. The dedication

Paul says in verse 36, "If any man [father] think that he

behaveth himself unseemly toward his virgin, if she pass the flower of her age, and need so require, let him do what he will, he sinneth not; let them marry." In light of teaching about the advantages of singleness, some of the fathers in Corinth had apparently dedicated their young daughters to the Lord as permanent virgins. But when the daughters became of marriageable age, many of them no doubt wanted to be married, and their fathers were in a terrible position. Should they break the vow they made for their daughters? The father may have realized that his daughter, having since reached the peak of her sexual maturity, truly desired to get married. It is likely that many of the girls did not have the gift of singleness. They were struggling with their desire to get married and their desire to please their father and the Lord. This problem was surely one of the questions the Corinthians had asked Paul in their first letter (7:1).

2. The decision

Paul says, "If she pass the flower of her age," that is, when she reaches sexual maturity "and need so require, let him do what he will, he sinneth not; let them marry" (v. 36). If a father made a vow for his daughter but realized he was not being fair because now she desired to be married, Paul said to let the daughter get married. The father may have had a noble aspiration, but the girl probably didn't have the gift of singleness. By implication, there must be a potential mate, because the text says, "Let *them* marry." Paul says the father was acting unfairly because he was putting his daughter in a potentially tempting situation. He would be running into the same problem that Jephthah had when he made a vow that ultimately killed his daughter (Judg. 11:29-40). A father who had vowed that his daughter would remain single to serve the Lord more devotedly was free to change his mind and allow her to marry if she needed to. After all, it was a vow made for someone else and was therefore subject to that person's spiritual needs. Just as unmarried people themselves are under no restraint (v. 35) and do not commit sin by marrying (v. 28), neither does a father who has made a vow do wrong by changing his mind.

3. The discovery

Paul discusses the opposite situation in verse 37: "Nevertheless, he that standeth steadfast in his heart, having no necessity, but hath power over his own will, and hath so decreed in his heart that he will keep his virgin, doeth well." Paul is saying that if the father has not changed his mind about his promise and is under no constraint by the daughter to change his mind, he will do well in having her remain single. If the daughter had no great strong sexual desire for marriage, it will be good for her to remain as she is. If the father has a pure motive—"hath power over his own will"—and is deeply committed "and hath so decreed in his heart," he may allow his daughter to remain unmarried for service and devotion to the Lord. Only the daughter's unwillingness to keep the vow should cause the father to change his mind. His steadfastness in his vow will encourage his daughter to be steadfast in hers. But if she does not have the gift for singleness, he may be doing her a bigger disservice by keeping her single. The key issue in verses 36-38 is one of advantage versus disadvantage. If the daughter is set on remaining single, she has a unique advantage in serving the Lord. But if she desires marriage, the father will do well in recognizing that and allow her to serve the Lord as a married person.

VI. THE PERMANENCY OF MARRIAGE (vv. 39-40)

"The wife is bound by the law as long as her husband liveth; but if her husband be dead, she is at liberty to be married to whom she will, only in the Lord. But she is happier if she so abide, after my judgment; and I think also that I have the Spirit of God."

This additional word about singleness is not tacked on to Paul's discussion, as some interpreters suggest. It focuses on the permanency of the marriage relationship.

A. The Focus

The focus of Paul's argument here is this: If your spouse dies and you are released from that marriage bond, you are better off if you remain single for full and complete devotion to Christ the rest of your life. "If you are deciding whether or not to marry," Paul says, "Remember that marriage is life-long." You will never be able to exercise the full potential of singleness once you marry. Because marriage is a lifelong commitment, think seriously before marrying. Although Christians with the gift of singleness are free to be married, they should keep in mind that if they marry, they are bound for the rest of their lives if they should die before their partner.

B. The Friendship

Now, please don't think I am down on marriage. I love my wife and children and would not have it any other way. Marriage is a wonderful opportunity for friendship and companionship. But those who have been specifically gifted by God for singleness need to consider the equally wonderful opportunity for unique service for Christ. If you choose to marry, you have given up the right to remain unmarried. Paul's words ring true for this chance to be especially committed to the plan of God.

C. The Fidelity

Paul says in verse 39, "If her husband be dead, she is at liberty to be married to whom she will, only in the Lord" (cf. 1 Cor. 9:5; Rom. 7:2). Death severs a marriage. The advice here is to widows and widowers. Widowed believers are not bound to stay single, but if they remarry it must be to another believer. There is no such thing as missionary dating. Christians are not to date or marry unbelievers. Deuteronomy 7:1-4 indicates that believers are to marry only those in the family of God (cf. 2 Cor. 6:14).

D. The Future

Paul takes one more opportunity to state his conviction on singleness: "[The widow] is happier if she so abide [in singleness], after my judgment." Paul again reiterates that remarriage is not the ideal; it is not God's best for everyone. He is not giving a command but is giving counsel for the benefit of those who take it. A woman who has God's grace for singleness will be happier if she remains single.

Conclusion

Paul ends the chapter by using a touch of sarcasm. He says, "And I think also that I have the Spirit of God." Paul was responding to those who were saying only they had the Spirit of God and were able to make right pronouncements. That statement doesn't serve to lessen Paul's point but to strengthen it. Both the Jewish and Gentile leaders were advocating philosophies that were contrary to sound doctrine—one advocating marriage only and the other advocating celibacy only. Paul was not merely giving opinion but divine revelation from the Lord Jesus Christ Himself. He was still speaking as "an apostle of Jesus Christ by the will of God" (1 Cor. 1:1, NASB). His conviction and his advice on singleness and marriage—and all other matters—is that of the Lord Himself.

Focusing on the Facts

1. Discuss what the Bible teaches concerning the design of marriage (see pp. 98-99).
2. How has the church tended to regard those who remained single (see p. 99)?
3. Single people are just as qualified for _____ _____ as those who are married (see p. 99).
4. Describe two different philosophies concerning marriage that were circulating around Corinth (see pp. 99-100).
5. The issue is not a person's marital status but his _____ (see p. 100).
6. True or false: Marriage is only a part of this world and will not occupy a place in heaven (see p. 101).
7. Describe what is meant by the preoccupations of marriage (see pp. 102-3).
8. True or false: The gift of singleness is the only spiritual gift that you have the option to use. Explain your answer (see p. 103).
9. Describe what is meant by this phrase: "That she may be holy both in body and in spirit" (v. 34; see p. 104).
10. What two motives did Paul have in mind in advising the Corinthians to remain single (see p. 105)?
11. What is the main point of the illustration from Mary and Martha in Luke 10 (see pp. 105-6)?
12. Describe what is meant by the fifth reason for remaining single, "The Promises of Fathers" (see pp. 106-7).
13. What was the cultural norm for marriage selections in the Old and New Testaments (see pp. 106-7)?
14. True or false: First Corinthians 7:36-38 is simply an historical account and is not applicable for fathers today (see p. 107).
15. Explain the options of a father regarding the marital status of his daughter (see pp. 108-9).
16. What one reason should lead a father to change his mind regarding his daughter's singleness (see p. 110)?
17. What are the main points Paul wanted to convey in verses 39-40 (see p. 110)?
18. Why did Paul use sarcasm in verse 40 (see p. 111)?

Pondering the Principles

1. The Lord Jesus Christ wants His children to have His undivided attention. One potential problem is the preoccupation of marriage. According to the apostle Paul in verses 32-35, it is a fact that those who are married will be preoccupied with each other. On that basis, Paul's conviction was that those who had the choice for singleness should exercise that option. Are you single? If so, you should consider Paul's advice to remain that way. If you are single and feel as though you do not have God's gift for singleness, you do not need to feel you are bound to remain unmarried. Thank God for your present situation, whatever it may be, and trust Him for your marital future.

2. In Jewish culture, parents long had a dominant role in deciding whom their children would marry. Although in Western society most young couples have freedom of choice concerning their partner, godly parents can have a tremendous influence on their children by their example and wisdom. If you have a son or daughter that will be making that decision soon, help your child to make the best decision he could possibly make. If he feels free of any sexual desire, he may have been gifted with God's grace for singleness. If so, encourage him to be all that God has intended for him as a single servant of the Lord.

3. Paul reiterates in verses 39-40 that a marriage relationship is lifelong. It is not to be entered into lightly. On that basis, those making that decision should evaluate the commitment required. It may be that singleness is the option for you. If you have been married in the past and your spouse has died, you are free to remarry. Realize however, that your singleness affords an unlimited potential for service to Christ. Carefully consider Paul's advice about your future. Ask God whether He would have you remain single for the sake of bringing others to the Savior who might not come otherwise. If it be so, thank God continually for giving you the gift of singleness. Use it for His glory.

Scripture Index